FOLLY

FOLLY

NADA GORDON

ROOF BOOKS
NEW YORK

ISBN 13: 978-1-931824-23-1
ISBN 10: 1-931824-23-1
Library of Congress Catalog Card Number: 2007921083

Cover art and illustrations: drawings by Gary Sullivan of collages by Nada Gordon, except for the the lambie on p. 123, which was collaboratively rendered by Coco Fitterman and Safia Fiera Biasia Mischka Lulu Romichke Karasick Southey. Cover color, author photo and book design by Nada Gordon.

Versions of these poems first appeared in *Abraham Lincoln, Combo, Lit, Vanitas, Shampoo, Magazine Cypress, EOAGH* and *Elsewhere*. Please accept my apologies if I have inadvertently left out any publications.

Quotations from *The Praise of Folly* by Desidirius Erasmus are drawn from the Barnes and Noble Books Edition, 2004, translated by John Wilson. The text for "Animal Act with Baboon..." comes from the following Web site: http://memory.loc.gov/cgi-bin/query/r?ammem/varstg:@field(NUMBER(4000)). Lines, forms, and concepts have been magpied from Della Crusta, Wilfred Owen, John, Ashbery, Frank O'Hara, and any number of other authors, many anonymous.

Affectionate thanks to Gary Sullivan, Rodney Koeneke, Tim Peterson, Benjamin Friedlander, Michael Gottlieb, as well as all the members of the Flarf Collective, whose ebullience is a constant buoy in a sea of inanity.

Roof Books are distributed by
Small Press Distribution
1341 Seventh Avenue
Berkeley, CA 94710-1403

Phone orders: 800-869-7553
www.spdbooks.org.

State of the Arts

NYSCA

This book was made possible, in part, with public funds from the New York State Council on the Arts, a state agency.

ROOF BOOKS
are published by
Segue Foundation
303 East 8th Street
New York, NY 10009
www.seguefoundation.com

~ for Sharon Mesmer ~

There are too many spelling or grammatical errors in Folly to continue
displaying them. To check the grammar and spelling of this document,
choose Spelling and Grammar from the Tools menu.

OK

nonsense, absurdity, craziness, daftness, dottiness, dumb trick, dumbo, fatuity, foolishness, idiocy, imbecility, impracticality, imprudence, inadvisability, inanity, indiscretion, irrationality, lunacy, madness, obliquity, preposterousness, rashness, recklessness, senselessness, silliness, stupidity, triviality, unsoundness, vice, witlessness, ridiculousness applesauce, bull, crap, craziness, farce, flapdoodle, folly, foolishness, hot air, idiocy, illogicality, illogicalness, improbability, inanity, incongruity, insanity, irrationality, jazz, jive, ludicrousness, ridiculousness, senselessness, silliness, stupidity, unreasonableness, escapade, adventure antic, caper, frolic, folly, frolic, gag, high jinks, lark, mischief, monkeyshines, prank, rib, roguery, rollick, romp, scrape, shenanigans, spree, stunt, trick, vagary extravagance indulgence, absurdity, amenity, dissipation, exaggeration, excess, exorbitance, expenditures, folly, frill, immoderation, improvidence, lavishness, luxury, outrageousness, over-indulgence, overdoing, overspending, preposterousness, prodigality, profligacy, profusion, recklessness, squander, squandering, superfluity, unreasonableness, unrestraint, unthrift, waste, wastefulness, wildness, foolishness, idiocy, absurdity, absurdness, bull, bunk, bunkum, carrying-on, claptrap, craziness, dumb trick, fiddle-faddle, fiddlesticks, folly, fool trick, foolery, fudge, horse feathers, impracticality, imprudence, inanity, indiscretion, insanity, insensibility, irrationality, irresponsibility, ludicrousness, lunacy, mistake, nonsense, poppycock, preposterousness, rubbish, senselessness, silliness, stupidity, tommyrot, twaddle, unreasonableness, unwiseness, weakness, witlessness freak, irregularity bee, caprice, conceit, crochet, fad, fancy, folly, humor, megrim, quirk, turn, twist, vagary, whim, whimsy frivolity silliness, childishness, coquetting, dallying, flightiness, flippancy, flirting, flummery, folly, fribble, foppery, frivolousness, fun, gaiety, game, giddiness, jest, levity, lightheartedness, lightness, nonsense, play, puerility, shallowness, sport, superficiality, toying, trifling, triviality, volatility, whimsicality, whimsy indiscretion mistake bloomer, blooper, bobble, booboo, boot, bullheadedness, bumble, crudeness, dumb trick, error, excitability, faux pas, foly, foolish mistake, foolishness, foul-up, gaffe, gaucherie, goof, hastiness, imprudence, indiscreetness, ingenuousness, lapse, louse, mistake, misjudgment, misspeak, muck up, naïveté, rashness, recklessness, screw up, simple-mindedness, slip, slipup, stumble, stupidity, tactlessness, thoughtlessness, unseemliness, insanity, foolishness, aberration, absurdity, alienation, craziness, delirium, delusion, dementia, derangement, distraction, dotage, folly, frenzy, hallucination, hysteria, illusion, inanity, irrationality, irresponsibility, lunacy, madness, mania, mental disorder, mental illness, neurosis, phobia, preposterousness, psychopathy, psychosis, senselessness, stupidity, unbalance, unreasonableness, witlessness, levity, funniness, absurdity, amusement, buoyancy, facetiousness, festivity, fickleness, flightiness, flippancy, folly, foolishness, frivolity, giddiness, grins, happiness, high spirits, hilarity, hoopla, jocularity, laughs, light-heartedness, mirth, picnic, pleasantry, repartee, silliness, trifling, triviality, volatility, whoopee, wit

～ Discontents ～

☀ Act One: An Ape in Purple Clothing

☀ Act Two: A Very Boring Society

☀ Intermission: Animal Diversions

☀ Act Three: A Dissonant Gaiety

# On Folly

The folly of mistaking a paradox for a discovery, a metaphor for a proof, a torrent of verbiage for a spring of capital truths, and oneself for an oracle, is inborn in us.

~ Paul Valery

Folly. We are all, I am sure, rife with her. I can think of no exception.

Folly tenderizes, renders us flabby and porous, milky monster-infants.

The word is an old-fashioned one. It differs from foolishness in that it is more neutral.

A folly can be absurdly entertaining (as in "Ziegfield's Follies") or can have very grave consequences.

However, war is not folly. War is bio-aggression deviously channeled by the State — a cold and vicious calculus. Although pressed into the service of war, Folly is not planned in rooms. She has an element of, if not spontaneity, incredible almost physical momentum.

She carries the person doing (committing? experiencing?) the folly along like an intoxication. So she's like gambling.

Sometimes folly is raveled up with power, the need to display or exercise it. All Trump buildings are follies. Bill Clinton is an archetypal walking male folly. Most arguments, I suspect, are follies (intoxicating, carrying-away) — particularly literary arguments. Erasmus says of writers that:

> sometime again they take up the cudgels, and challenge out an antagonist, and so get a name by a combat at dispute and controversy, while the unwary readers draw sides according to their different judgments: the longer the quarrel holds the more irreconcilable it grows; and when both parties are weary, they each pretend themselves the conquerors, and both lay claim to the credit of coming off with victory. These fooleries make sport for wise men, as being highly absurd, ridiculous and extravagant.

A person who commits a folly may be paradoxically, and sometimes simultaneously, derided and admired by other people because a folly is a kind of break with expectation. When expectation is broken, we see the little sparks that remind us we are alive. Sometimes the little sparks are pure acid that eats through decorum.

Unlike mere foolishness, Folly has an element of gaiety and abandon. In gaiety and abandon the borders of appropriateness can be transgressed, and there are consequences. But the lack of premeditation in an act of folly also points to the folly-doer's lack of foresight.

A carousel is always a folly, at least architecturally. Gary and I were walking through Prospect Park yesterday, a truly verdant spring day overflowing with forsythia and cherry blossoms, past the carousel, whereupon I made the comment that carousels make me cry, and not merely over "spent youth" although there is that, too. The folly of a carousel is the folly of life: lugubrious, sporadically hyperactive, ultimately terminal.

Oh and then we came home, and — kismet! — Gary happened to put on a Bollywood film, *Mela*, which means "The Fair." Black and white, village imagery, little handcranked ferris wheels, girls in saris riding by on oxcarts, and a guy with remarkable teeth singing a moody song in Hindi... ah, *ukiyo*...

Once, sitting on a bench outside the Central Park carousel with Masaya on a visit from Japan several years ago, I wept inconsolably, thinking of my first love. Masaya put his arm around me, relishing the poignancy of that moment as *fuel for haiku*. He was a strange man with a keen sense of folly.

Folly's a pretty word, she dances on the tongue, she wears a beaver top hat with bells on it. She tattooes stocking seams upon her naked legs. She is insidious, a cabaret snake. She puts up buildings and knocks them down. She is responsible for huge flows of capital, language, and bodily fluids.

Folly — ubiquitous as air and twice as toxic. With her thoughtless power, she pierces the styrofoam rocks, tumbles them down. Folly as phoenix rustles her chiming tail, her garnet eyes spinning like teacups...

Folly. Folllllllllly. Falalalala...

# Whate'er

after Erasmus

Here in lively color lies
a discharge, exposed and virgin naked
like a jerk, or pent-up
like a fold of sleep
or smatch of peevish pelf
that justles, kicks, and tumbles
o'er the modern satyrs of the arts
whose opiated milk glues up
the brain like glittering hair
on blowsy grapes.

This all's a sacrifice
of salt and fire, doctrine-
dangling and hoisted in a fright.
The bawdy subject — a croaking
prawn or snick'ring ape,
tongue guided by wit — alters
all the texts (transform'd to swine),
and wonders thus at men,
and chafes the words,
bold and loud like cocks —
and so foments desire.

List of Characters:

Folly
Flarfalini
Omanko
Florenz Ziegfeld
Desidirio Erasmus
Ira Gershwin
Bill Clinton
Gary
Masaya
Helen
Asha Bhosle
Pippy
Elizabeth
Jessica
Jennifer
Duala
Cindy
A.L.
Julie
Jeni
Martia
Cassie
Katlyn
Amy
Sarah
Narisa
Nila
Gretchen
Alicia
Lilac
Chris
Monica
Shaina
Anonymous
Paranoid
Scared
Terrified
Milton Berle
Cher
Heloise

Anarkali
Juliet
Barbarian
Bass de Soie
Born Too Late
Buttonitis
Buxom Fiddler
Creak-lover
Hairpin
Horsey Typist
Lady Godiva
Louis Quinze
Little White Wasp
Lens Lover
Human Eel
Modern Victorian
Much Bored
Rainbow
Taut Boy
Would-be Eleven
    (inches)
Newscaster
Kent Johnson
Sheptanya
Brianna
Lovetta
a clerk
NothingKitty
Auntie BamBam
Snuggles
Parameter
    (a kitty)
Diogenes
    (a parrot)
Phelicity
Sweet Kitty
Hot Miko
Wild Hazmy
Urban Barbie
Barbara Eden

Guava
Blurty
Ann-Margret
Pluto
Tiki
Han Xiangzi
Marduk
Venus
Arawn
God
Boota Ili
Amaterasu
Kali
Beelzebub
Allah
Star-Shaped
    Pillowcase
Fat Thing
Rusty Helmet
Earthquake
The Skull on
    the President
Bunnies
Hummingbirds
Peacocks
George W.
    Bush
Ahnold
Condoleezza
Rummy
Liberace
Cheney
Ashcroft
Lucifer
Starsailor
Miss America
Peggy Noonan
Mariko Mori
Wilfred Owen
Krystal

Emma Lazarus
Loquacious the Snail
Melissa, a chameleon
Mr. Fucko, a hamster
James Sherry
Nada
piglet of ignonymity
Hector
Rasputin
The Bagelman Sisters
Shelly Winters
Gumby
Pokey
Sparklechick
Universal Hominid
Ancestor
Imelda Marcos
Sunny Pain
Bernie Goetz
Bodhisattva
Goat
Breast
Seraph
Milk Emanation
Wolf-Fish
Shamrock Pea
Proudleduck
Capricorn
Milk Ferret
Wax Doll
Tasmanian Emu
Dark-Rumped Petrel
Little Bittern
Bourbon-pink Pigeon
Small-Billed False
Sunbird
Bird of Providence
Night Parrot
Long-Legged Warbler

Orange-Breasted Flowerpecker
Cherry-Throated Tanager
Rothschild's Grackle
Hemignathus Obscurus Obscurus
Sandhya
Sadhana
W.D. Snodgrass
Ann Lauterbach
Sapphire
Muriel Rukuyser
Mark Strand
Claudia Rankine
Mary Oliver
W.S. Merwin
Peter Gizzi
Sharon Olds
Cora Pearl
Mogador
Anonymous dancer of the Ouled Nail
Froufrou
Lucille Ball
Namie Amuro
Emilienne d'Alençon
Gracie Allen
Marie du Plessis
Monica Lewinsky
Appolonie Sabatier
The pink rabbits of Emilienne d'Alençon
Franz Kafka
Kazim al Saher
Anne Waldman
Cecilia Vicuña
A student
William Blake
Your name here: _____

ACT ONE:
An Ape in Purple Clothing

Now that which made Plato doubt under what genus to rank woman, whether among brutes or rational creatures, was only meant to denote the extreme stupidness and Folly of that sex, a sex so unalterably simple, that for any of them to thrust forward, and reach at the name of wise, is but to make themselves the more remarkable fools, such an endeavor, being but a swimming against the stream, nay, the turning the course of nature, the bare attempting whereof is as extravagant as the effecting of it is impossible: for it is a trite proverb: *That an ape will be an ape, though clad in purple*; so a woman will be a woman, i.e., a fool, whatever disguise she takes up.

~ Desidirius Erasmus

Baubles, bangles,
Hear how they jing, jing-a-ling-a,
Baubles, bangles,
Bright, shiny beads.
Sparkles, spangles,
My heart will sing, sing-a-ling-a,
Wearing baubles, bangles and beads.

~ Ira Gershwin

I am the princess of my feelings and the queen of my mind. Girls today have reached the moon. Don't be guilty of blasphemy. Was that really you or was it a luminous sunbeam, a blossoming bud, a monsoon?

Nail Art: stimulating five senses

She denied the concept that a nail art is only superficial on fingertips.

Anyone has his/her personality, expectations and hopes at the moment.

You can make those images realities that spring up in the inner side.

By representing their fitting color or shapes, it enables to see your new status.

Those perfect and sentient representations are not only about the micro-world to express the delicate, but also about the macro-world, which deeply fascinates your eyes when you see.

What about turning your fingertips into the panel?

Why don't you getting only one art in the world?

baubles and
bangles and
baubles
and bangles and baubles and bangles and
baubles and bangles
and baubles and bangles and baubles and baubles and baubles and baubles and

      baaaaangles
         and
             b   a
                u
                   b
                  l
                   e
                 s

Vagabond Imperialism

[Folly, as herself, fanning her plumes:]

Who isn't envaginated in rhetoric?
Slathered with its perfume, pigs root through
the debris of the 20th century — a scuttling octopus,
a spidery machine, ghosts of ocean rays. Here's an octave
and a cup of bitters, some kohlrabi, and creepy
music-box music. **POP**! Out come the same old
arguments leading to the same old cul de sacs, then **POP**
they all disappear in a shower of gluey sparks, like extreme
plastic surgery performed on sponge-y homunculae.

At least Gaptoothed Helen dances to the level of her eyeliner.
And Asha Bhosle, in a mirrored choli,
lets loose with the heavy breathing,
as lusty as a bacon hog, or sucking calf.

*they garnish themselves with paint, washes, perfumes,
and all other mysteries of ornament*

Abnormal Discharge

pill question? …medication… pippy
sex hurts :(
cuts and labia irritation
necessary to take all placebo pills?
wierd white/yellowish vaginal discharge
High Viscosity in Sperm
possible pregnecy Elizabeth
possible pregnecy
vaginal discharge Jessica
Abnormal Pap Smear Jennifer
Abnormal Pap
Vaginal Itching and Peeling anon
Vaginal Itching and Peeling
chlamydia thru blood transfusion?
vagina size paranoid
vagina size
vagina size anonymous
bleeding after intercourse pippy
Breast Pimples (Professional, please)
White spots on breast Duala
White spots on breast anonymous
Duala White spots on breast anonymous
White spots on breast anonymous
White spots on breast
Could it be a cyst?
Vagina 'bumps' Duala
Vagina 'bumps' anonymous
Vagina 'bumps' anonymous
ovarian pains Jessica
ovarian pains anonymous
Painful intercourse Curious
Painful intercourse net
Brownish Redish discharge.
Amoxicillin and Depo Provera anonymous
My Period has been done for 5 days !! now have
thick brown creamy like discharge can anyone
help me out? Cindy
can hand warts lead to gential warts? A.L.
Did I have a possible miscarriage? Julie

Did I have a possible miscarriage?
Worries about 'down there' — scared terrified
Worries about 'down there' — scared anonymous
vaginal itching and swelling
Pink Stuff Anonymous
VERY SCARED should i be worried about this? Jeni
VERY SCARED should i be worried about this? martia
VERY SCARED should i be worried about this? jeni
VERY SCARED should i be worried about this? Cassie
Blood Clot? Worried
Fibroids Janice
Fibroids
air in vagina db
air in vagina anonymous
air in vagina amy
No Period! Katlyn
No Period!
oral sex sara
oral sex
Nervous Wreck anonymous
Nervous Wreck
Average sagging?
Average sagging?
Average sagging?
breast discharge — again irene
breast discharge — again Marisa Geller MD
Types of Vaginas??? Nila
Types of Vaginas??? Gretchen
Types of Vaginas??? Marisa
Weird discharge
Weird discharge Alicia
White bump near anus Cindy
White bump near anus
Weird period!! help!!! Lilac
Weird period!! help!!!
What's going on here? Monica
way to orgasm?
way to orgasm? Jessica
Unusual question regarding problems with orgasm Chris
What is this???? Shaina
Considering Partial Hysterectomy Shaina
Considering Partial

genital appearances anonymous

Womanish

Milton Berle: You are acting like a big woman.

Erasmus: It didn't matter that he behaved like a freak and there is no need for either person to try and control each other.

Milton Berle: You are acting womanish ARE YOU A FREAK? Womanish creature! Now, let it go now give the Holy Ghost control now.

Ziegfeld: We like to call our young girls womanish of freaks — mannish women and womanish men. Nocturnal order.

Erasmus: Meaning given by a dictionary of *womanish* is "of Devil, Dog, Drone, Dwarf, Fever, Freak, Hawk, Hell."

All: Together we stand, divided we freak out.

Milton Berle: Ridiculed as "sentimental," "impractical," or "womanish," I hadn't quite expected to make a womanish sound. I bit my lip and turned my head,until I thought I had enough control to speak.

Erasmus: A freak begins, and a freak abandons himself to useless outcries and womanish lamentations.

The judge within the breast can control this extreme infantine intellect — the variable animals — like a woman indeed indulging in her own womanish and tender state of being faint.

All: *flimflam* n. A freak; a trick

Porpo-Thang

The porpoises fling up their
orange underthings; swaying
in the wind, their heavy rotation
is brief and horrifying,

full of bright scrawls, of thin
and lacy garters.
There isn't a place
in this world that doesn't

sooner or later drown
in the porridge of upload.
But now, for a while,
the bustier

shines like an undertaker
as it floats above everything
with its yellow cognitive science.
Of course, nothing stops the flimsy,

black, curved porousness
from bending forward —
of course,
restlessness is the great undertone.

But I also say this: that thongs
are an invitation
to undervaluation,
and that undervaluation,

when it's done right,
is a kind of porousness,
palpitating and porphyritic.
Inside the tight fields,

touched by their rough and spongy noises,
I am washed and washed
in the porridge
of satin delight—

and what are you going to do—
what *can* you do
about it—

flung, orange negligée?

Chains, coronets, pendans, bracelets and earrings,
Pins, girdles, spangles, embroideries and rings;
Shadoes, rebaltoes, ribbands, ruffs, cuffs, falls,
Scarfes, feathers, fans, maskes, muffs, laces, cauls;
Thin tiffanies, cobweb lawn, and fardingals,
Sweet fals, vayles, wimples, glasses, crisping pins;
Pots of ointments, combes, with poking sticks and bodkins,
coyfes, gorgets, fringes, rowles, fillets and hair-laces;
Silks, damasks, velvet, tinsels, cloth of gold,
Of tissues with colours of a hundred fold.

~ Ralph Knevet, *Rhodon and Iris*, 1631

Soapy Erection

[*shower of cotton balls in the pornotopiary*]

Heloise: Springy, silky hirsute plunge, a mouthed apricot
             kernelling the loops inside a listless tongue. Its swollen
             fever mauve as pollen, lit globes of syrup movement spin
             so fast I'm going to fall off the wonder harpy's magic
             brainstem again. The pseudo-electric lights there like
             morays and heart's heaving blizzard effects a blizzard of
             cilia and algae struck to a wandering hand — whoops!
             whoops on the wind, gripping what's being ridden to
             starry deeps, strummed as a hinge, thrummed through
             bilkings and coughs and furtive imagined clefts of
             milkweed seed.

             Boobie water gun

             dicky sipping straws

             peckertoss

             peni-nails

             hard core preggy pantie fixed cheese omelettes!

[*rattling foil*]

Anarkali: "Do you have milk?" says the pretty ingenue to the
             jockey erect on his steed, spine as straight as desire is a
             ruse for life as it can only be lived — to make throaty
             signals to the drummers covered with almond powder,
             farfisas swirling on the pendulous sac. Fish eggs! Fish
             eggs! Flickering lustre! The stud — the strudel's — on
             the bottom and the pie's in your hair, nipping at the
             flared lips of the stallion's sensibilities. Woo! Woo!
             Woowee! Empurplement. The short lives of lilies and
             their saffron stamens — oops — I got it all over my
             nipple again in the broad distance I call "gentle" or
             "glorious" or "I really shouldn't jinx it" depending on my
             lord's mood, his apple-y stomach stroked with gel like

something burned from the inside out: spilled milk,
spilled milk, spilled milk. Nandi the cow lies down on
the rose petal, the houri emerges in musky garments,
pink and blue birds flutter in mating.

Mr America Walking Pecker

dickyboppers

strawberry pulsabath

dick through the head

[*mazurka-like hoop jumping of pink rabbits — sprays of honey powder*]

Juliet: Spring! Kiss me, sweet William, bright orange egg,
flicker, flicker, little snail, flared out like adrenaline
rubbed all over with lanolin and fur. Sparking crevices
and full bursting to a droop. Sea of mung, ornamental
pepper, weigh down the bee-loud trellis with your
frabjous jamjar hand!

koochie pencil sharpener

amazing growing pecker — from wee-wee to
whopper!

The mussels and their lips, the greeny membranes,
the flat apricot clams.

Moistly fluttering up to the explosion of oh!!! feathers
falling in twitchy heavings on my purple stockings,
sweet with crotch musk aching in blossoms.

His lips that licking my folded claspings send up
through the nerves puffs of melody from my painted
mouth.

Oily nipple, thrill of entry. Contacting tongues to
activate the hearts, dual doumbeks in the craving
room.

❧ I Love Men

Barbarian:

I wrote the meanest, silliest thing below about men. I'm so sorry. Please ignore.

Bas de Soie:

Anyway, here's why I love men. They are brave. I love men's thighs, their hands; the small of their necks; I love men. But more than the physicality of it all, I love that men are freaks — born.

Born Too Late:

I love men. And that's why it bothers me — no, "infuriates" would be a better word…

Buttonitis:

I love men for their strength. Sometimes it is that vein that bulges on the upper part…
I love men for the way they give up everything but themselves for love.

Buxom Fiddle:

I love men with big penis… and I love men's hair. Everything about men's hair is a wonder to me… I love men who come to me once every two months with thick dark hair in their nostril.

Creak-lover:

I love men. I love mean ones, and nice ones, and fat ones, and skinny ones. But most of all, I love super-hot ones.
The sensation of pooh in my mouth.

Hairpin:

I LOVE TO HANG OUT WITH MY FRIENDS AND GO TO PARTIES I LIKE ALOT OF SEQUENCE OF CLOTHING I LOVE MEN WITH GOOD PERSONILITY

Horsey Typist:

I love men in cycling shorts… I love men in kilts, I love men with long legs. I love men who are pigeon toed. I… I just…
love men. I love stripping men naked with just my eyes. It's something that I want all the time now. And I mean ALL THE TIME.

I love men who are slightly cocky
and arrogant... something sexy there...

Lady Godiva: Urgh, I love men with top hats and beautifully
tailored tuxedos and immaculately polished shoes.
I Love Men In Uniform I Love Men In Uniform
Charm. I Love Firemen I Love Firemen Charm.
I love men in turbans.
I love men who wear fishnet and skirts. It's just
downright sexy.
I love men staring from buses in the next lane.
Sometimes, my boyfriend will make me go out in a
miniskirt without panties
to go on an escalator.

Louis Quinze: I Love Men in Boots! That's a whole lotta boots!

Little White Wasp: I love men, but they wear me out with all their
confusing issues. One day they say they love you and
the next they see someone with bigger ass.

Lens-Lover: I love men, muscles, sex, porn, and chocolate.

Human Eel: I Love Men on Prozac. I love men on Prozac with
their calm, James Dean smiles and dreamy novelist
eyes.

Modern Victorian: Of course I love men of all races... but, I have to
admit I am completely fascinated by Asian men.
Japanese, Chinese, Korean... I love it all.

Much Bored: I love men. They are energetic, great at fetching and I
love them.
Darlings. I love men, especially when they are silent,
beautiful and have no panties.

Rainbow: I LOVE WIENERS And Jewels I love men Money
Power And I love my sex Me and My sex And I love
my sex Only Me and My sex La la la la la la la la la.

Taut Boy: I love men, even though they're
                lying, cheating scumbags. I love men,
                not for what unites them, but for what divides
                them, and I want to know most of all what
                gnaws at their hearts.

Would-Be Eleven
(inches):   I LOVE MEN!!! I LOVE MEN!!! I LOVE
                MEN!!! I LOVE MEN!!! I LOVE MEN!!!
                I LOVE MEN!!! I LOVE MEN!!! I LOVE
                MEN!!! I LOVE MEN!!!
                I LOVE MEN!!!
                I LOVE MEN!!

Orgone Gophers

Cooing pop huckles. Minarlagy of funf. The latter craal-skeevers
(anxious like bucket): froos, angle, insecure.

I keen my meringo this hopey day. I murv it. The hopcakes are waiting
for the nested parlances, the nested parlances for a
6-month grace period, after which they will expire.

It all comes together as perforations in the ample slough —
beastborne, tolerant, mint, and gland-handed.

Where's my speed, the clock's a muffle, the clown raises sham
hackles, the plain stripes badger the nonplain stripes as limits to
patience.

The men hack outside the door in explicatory gasses. They muddle
and wink, halving their trousers. The parts rattle by in pink bones.
The men are wuthering. A stag wuthers the hard waiting.

The men lift up the thorny leaves of togetherness.
There is a pad there.

Under the pad, another man, horning a thought as a drawing.
The pink ones wonder — bastard hardcake? Terrible wuthering
intertwining a lumpy duddle.

The plaid couches, pro dusk and anti-dawn, haunched by men
and soaky weapons like flags rolled up in glands while the plaid
maidens change their lamb sprockets.

Inches and inches and inches of man, boozling and edgily nuzzling.
Fungible playthings! Limbering the cud. Sweat drapes. Miracle
sinews absolute the free fibers of a flexibly ordered man, half red
and half blue, on a night watch and skin patrol.

I don't can't — can't can't — a man. Hip dud. Catafrack. Pone.

༜ The Dressing Room

Newscaster
Kent Johnson
Sheptanya
Brianna
Lovetta
Dressing Room Attendant

Newscaster: The December boom is a boon for many stores, and heavy sales are often posted across the board. Even corporate juggernauts depend on the sales boost from end-of-the-year holidays.

                    Kent Johnson, executive team leader of Hard Lines for the Lawrence SuperTarget, has managed the "In Season" department of the store in the past, and he knows the amount of work required to make it all run smoothly.

Kent Johnson: The December days are nearly double. It's not uncommon to do almost twice as much business.

Newscaster: So says Johnson, a Nebraska native and a nine-year employee of Target. When your customer count increases from 4,000 to 8,000 per day (as Johnson estimates it does for Target), the logistics of maintaining high-quality service multiply quickly.

[*Enter Brianna, Lovetta, and Sheptanya with their arms full of clothing to try on. Newscaster approaches them with a microphone.*]

                    Ladies, what do you look for when you shop at Target?

Brianna: Hmm. Bleached light elks — with wings. Pink leotards. Horns.

Lovetta: This internality, the pattern that is I, the agency of the self.

Sheptanya: For me, I guess... Elvis hair, Elvis glasses... homemade capes using a material with images of Elvis all over it...

Newscaster: Ahh…

[*the women march towards the dressing room, shoving the newscaster aside*]

Attendant: Just make sure to bring everything back on a hanger, k?
                You can go right in. It's communal.

Lovetta: [*disdainfully*] Communal. There is internality only with reference
                to the externality. If the externality goes away, where is the
                internality?

Attendant: Whatever. Just bring everything back on a hanger.

[*Inside the dressing room*]

Brianna: Meaning of humpy. What does humpy mean?

Sheptanya: Humpy the Dog. I don't know what it is about dogs
                humping that tickles me, but it just does. This little
                Chihuahua is horny and needs to get fixed quick.

Lovetta: Humpy shrimp. Get me my leotard, leg warmers, and big
                hair wig. I'm off to the gym!

Sheptanya: There is always a tiny version of you in a tight red leotard
                and horns

Lovetta: Yep, that's what I am… humpy. And sooo not in a sexual
                way. So, not only am I humpy, my off-kilter hips will
                eventually cause me to be gimpy. Terrific!

Brianna: In a past life, Humpy was my name. Why my owner named
                me so is an interesting story While my other camel friends
were Shahrukh and Raveena, I was Humpy.

Sheptanya
and Lovetta: Harrumph!

[*Throughout the rest of the play the women try on outfits and comment on
their own and others' outfits.*]

Sheptanya:	How does this look?
Brianna:	Hmm. Make a claw hand.
Sheptanya:	Like this?
Brianna:	No, like this — look. The movement is as if you were scratching you belly in a circular fashion. The knuckles stay bent in the same position... kind of... full of humps or bunches; covered with protuberances; humped...
Sheptanya:	I think this makes me look like I am a punishment.
Lovetta:	No, it makes you like one bad muthafucka. How does this look on me?
Brianna:	[*getting up close and examining her critically*] A bra made of algae? Eww! Eww! Dude Seriously! This ain't a camel toe!!! It's the whole fuckin CAMEL FOOT!!!!!! LOL, it's devouring her leotard!
Lovetta:	Honey, he saw my cameltoe then canceled his wedding day. I bet Hannibal Lecter has the camel toe mouse pad!
Sheptanya:	Eww get away from me you preteen skank eww eww eww eww eww eww eww eww eww eww eww eww eww eww eww eww eww eww eww eww eww eww eww eww eww eww eww eww eww eww eww eww eww eww eww eww eww eww eww eww
Brianna:	Shush. I'm currently wearing a beanie (sans pompom) underneath my helmet, but sadly this makes me look even more like a complete penis-head
Lovetta:	This makes me look either a) retarded, or b) like a frightened horse about to bolt.
Sheptanya:	This makes me look askance at the contemporary mythology of the potential of a blessed and peace-filled utopia under the benevolent gaze of a mother goddess. I act violently because I feel angry (I am in pain) and this makes me look strong. What's strong is my charade.

Brianna: It's wild how tiny this makes me look. I'm shedding all my exhibitions.

Lovetta: Do you want my candied opinion? Frankly, I think you look ridorkulous in that gorilla suit.

Brianna: I Spit on Your Saint-emilion true-souled age-old fresh-watered pelican flower Lifestyle.

Lovetta: I spit on your rudeness at the store, at your throwing sulphur-tinted sodium chloride mist-enshrouded fermentation tubes on the floor.

Sheptanya: I spit on your spit.

Brianna: I Spit on Your Concrete worse-bodied stomach-ache pollen-covered wine-merry provost marshal Christ-taught swelled-gelatin process.

Sheptanya: If I spit on your food, is that annoying?

Lovetta: I Spit On Your fatal-looking brain-smoking watercress-y Robot.

Brianna: I Spit On Your dull-red Foam.

Lovetta: Do you mean "I spit on your soul" as an insult?

Brianna: I spit on your quasi power Siculo-punic bull fiddle snow pigeon christian ground I split your enormous lies I rape and ruin your holy land...

Sheptanya: You shall cry as I spit on your cross Bleed!!! You shall bleed for me as I tear off your wings Scream!!! You shall scream as I slowly crush your skull...

Lovetta: I spit on your logic and Pseudo-angle Ku-klux appraisal ability.

Sheptanya: I spit on your spam.

Brianna: I spit on your flat-cheeked "patriotism." It is as phony as phony gets.

Lovetta:	Pshaw. I spit on your philistine warm-complexioned beard faces. PTOOOOIE
Brianna:	I said to Saddam Hussein: "You despicable man, I spit on your owl's face. How do you address these glorious women without me knowing about it?"
Lovetta:	And we will say,
All:	"I spit on your flowers!"
Lovetta:	And you will say,
Sheptanya:	"But I worship you — I adore you. You are an angel."
Lovetta:	And we will say,
All:	"Yes, that's true!"
[pause]	
Sheptanya:	I spit on your irrelevance.
Brianna:	Poetry often enters through the window of irrelevance.
Lovetta:	[lyrically] Irrelevance fills my mind; unrelated, disembodied experiences rush forth!
Brianna:	Crippled by the sense of our own cultural irrelevance, we now write poems:

Sheptanya: [*clears throat — reciting in "poetry" mode*]

"Irrelevance"

Negation is mine
Under the shadow of you I eat me away…
"life is no cabaret"
earlobe looks like a camel-toe
Found a fun pair of French Kitty pajamas
fetish treasonous leotard fetish sock
This internality, this pattern that is I,
is the agency of the self
Probing the secrets of sticky earwax.

[*silence*]

Lovetta: You look real cute in that ninja getup.

Brianna: And may I just say you look delicious in that sari, you wicked thing. The original exposed midrift, how very charming indeed.

Sheptanya: This makes me look like Queen Victoria on a bad day.

Lovetta: Are you kidding? You look totally shaggable in that. I mean, you look cute in that "OMG, that girl has got some balls to wear THAT in public" way. At least you didn't have to wear elf ears.

Brianna: Does this make me look fickle? Or versatile?

Lovetta: Versatile. Does this make me look two-dimensional? Or careerist?

Sheptanya: Careerist. Does this make me look gelatinous? Or like slightly less of an awesomely intimidating authority figure?

Brianna: I think it makes you look "published." Does this make me look like I'm searching for an orange? Or too much like a road? Or do I just look dead?

Lovetta: "You look ravenous in that sweater." Hee-hee-hee…
oh lordy, you look goofy in that outfit — like some nude
Oregon cheerleader thrusting her borderline cameltoe in
our faces whilst straddling a cannon.

Sheptanya: This makes me look very sad, I realize. By the way, do
camels really spit?

Brianna: They aren't actually spitting — it's more like throwing
up! They bring up the contents of their stomachs, along
with saliva.

Lovetta: [*pedantically*] Definition of *spit*: *spit up*, to vomit; throw
up: The wounded soldier *spat up* blood. If you jostle the
baby, she'll *spit up*.

Sheptanya: pink floid pink floyd pink humpy pink 20% humpy

Brianna: Against the New Paternalism: Internalities and the
Economics of Camel Toe

Sheptanya: 12. DROON — cripplefight 13. CHEVRON — power
of eternia

Lovetta: High on head cement, eh? What is the best and worst
things about being a woman or man? Saliva, also known
as spit, is a clear liquid that's made in your mouth.

Brianna: Eyeball Lollipops

Sheptanya: Fluffy Humpy Poopy Puppy

Lovetta: He can feel the sweat-soaked Lycra of her leotard in his
embrace.

ALL: verb (past participle *spit* or *spat*,
present participle *spit*·ting)…
spit it out to say something at once,
especially something that has been withheld.

[*All women exit wearing strange new outfits and carrying armfuls of rejected
clothing — not on hangers — that they toss playfully at the clerk.*]

She Sure Likes the Cream *or* The Pink Rabbits of Emilienne d'Alençon

Sayonara fleurdelys.
Adieu, cherry twinklemall.
Human hair and glass EYES princess —
mischief kreme.

I have DREAM(s)! dreamy-girl
Magic the kitty cat Sweet Kitty!
Paper Panache paper-piecing patterns
My Dog Spot/ Sweet Kitty Dreams.
My Dog Spot/ Sweet Kitty Dreams.

Shiva Cat Slave to the Dance Sweet-Kitty.
[The Pink Power] Cliques: *Meu
What a SWEET kitty! What a SWEET kitty!
Darling little cathead with a pretty little bow
around its neck. Three Sweet Kitty Babies
NothingKitty acting like a SWEET Kitty

NothingKitty acting like a sweet
Human hair and glass eyes, SWEET KITTY
He is a sweet kitty, but can also be rather moody.
Sweetie is exactly that — a very sweet kitty.
Aww, Sweet Kitty. Oh My GOD!

Come pet my kitty sweet kitty
Yes, those with empathy are like kitties
you're nice you care Kitties are nice electric ferret
DOES YOUR SWEET KITTY LOOK AT YOU LIKE
THIS WHEN ASKED TO OBEY? MyLittle Kitty
This is my sweet kitty Shadow, finding Ugly
in Wolf, a reminder of our mortality.

Tuffy dog purrs all the time.
My dear Auntie BamBam, I love you TOO,
from Phelicity Sweet Kitty. Snuggles. This is Snuggles.
Won't YOU let me show YOU how sweet I am?

I am a very sweet kitty who is a little on the shy side.
I really am quite stunning.
I like to pose in front of the camera
and to show my body on the net...
Kitty, lose myself in your cotton fur.
Good kitty. Put me to sleep with your Nice kitty

Sweet Kitty Kiss my ghosts. Kitty doesn't like
the soup, Mama, but *she sure likes the cream*.
Sweet kitty, where'd she go? Scratchy tongue
and tiny wet nose. Sweet kitty, where you been?
Mares. Tijuana Pine Tijuana Moonshine Lady Sugar
Blue Bubbles. Come kitty kitty Come home

sweet kitty Come my sweet little Kitty
Come home sweet kitty Come to me Kitty kitty.
SWEET KITTY, HOT MIKO, WILD HAZMY.
SWEET KITTY, HOT MIKO, WILD HAZMY.
My sweet kitty Parameter, my parrot Diogenes,

Kitty, O Kitty, Your sweet more than the rest.
Kitty, sweet kitty. Your simply the best.
ANXIETY ATTACK! ANXIETY ATTACK!
to be entirely stable. Sweet sweet kitty,
until she decides she's not
and lets you know it.

Urban Barbie

I HATE MYSELF FOR SLEEPING!

1. This Isn't The Tenka-ichi Budokai. 2. Urban Barbie. 3. Polar Bear Summer. 4. And Keep Reaching For Those Stars.

Pung, Stressface. poopooloo. crescent. neutral. pink. paint me pink. school. backstabbers. pure blood bitches.

I hate myself... because I am utterly unable... [*Folly stumbles, wobbling on permanent tiptoes*]

[*enter Desidirio Erasmus in pantaloons*]
> You's not fat — you's curvaceous and voluptuous,
> and there ain't much wrong
> wit dat.

[*exit Erasmus*]

[*Folly resumes her song*]

I hate myself for being such a wimp.

I hate myself! I'm not looking for sympathy, in fact, just the opposite.

... and I hate the world we live in, because its all about how you look. and i think I look like shit. and I hate myself for thinking that. I know I shouldnt care.

I hate myself... I hate myself for looking pretty, I hate myself for being silly, I hate myself for covering it up, I hate it all, my life's fucked up.

I Hate Myself, Honesty. Why is it that I am such
an impossible person to love? I guess I apparently make things...

Vacuously Impermanent

[Installation: enormous pile of false eyelashes.]

Mother of heaven, *habibi*, don't you feel
intensely uncomfortable? Welter of blushes,
black steel carking spirit — the warped limbs
of profit. Machines empty their juices
in burgeoning conflict; girlies get surly
in mixups. Red origami garbage's electronically bad
easter face, like so much unread legislation.
The fact that tissue can inflame…
the chickadees. Throatrack — gorge —
it's sweet down here, underneath the truth.
Nothing like taking a break from lovemaking
and returning to the bed with sighs,
or waiting for the train the morning after
someone new.

My Eternal Dilemma

[*As sung by Folly and Folly's conjoined twin, Wisdom, who bears a strong resemblance to Barbara Eden morphed with Fanny Brice as played by Barbra Streisand. Musical accompaniment: anything heavily synthesized. Folly tries to comfort Wisdom but mostly the two girls just flop around uselessly in a cloud of dust motes and minute feathers. Costumes: three sequins.*]

Wisdom: My Eternal Dilemma… I think I have ADD. And no one loves me. And I annoy my friends a lot. And no one loves me. And I think I'm starting to hate men.

Folly: O Guava, why they don't notice me. Why I can't tell them how I feel. Why no one loves me. And no matter how hard I try, they'll never see.

Wisdom: I often feel that no one loves me. If I have problems, I have to tackle them on my own. At the moment, I feel like an outcast.

Folly: I only do these things because no-one loves me and my life is dull.

Wisdom: No one loves, me's Blurty.

Folly: [*holding hands up to face*] No one loves me like my tomato can.

Wisdom: This is the level of philosophies, conclusions, and assumptions, such as, "No one loves me."

Folly: Who can understand me if I can't understand my self? No one cares for me. No one loves me. I don't love my self. I am the dust swept under the rug.

Wisdom: Runaway. I want to runaway. But where would I go? No one would take me in, no one loves me. I could not stay on the streets.

Folly: SPORK, punkbunnypopsicle, punkbunnypopsicle, I'm lonely, no one loves me

Wisdom:	[*hands outstretched to audience*] Daddy! NO one LOVES ME!!!" The Wiseman says, "You must take revenge on them… using the power of the Dark Crystal!" Suddenly, the black rings enclose on her.
Folly:	[*twirling parasol*] I want a family, I want friends, I want everything that I don't have, I am a blue Elephante, I am blue because I am sad, No one loves me.
Wisdom:	You have Chocobo Ghost to love you! [*looks all innocent and hurt*] Unlike me… no-one loves me…
Folly:	And I want your input on this one, too… PWEASE? SORRY! Whatever, NO one loves me…? but some nectarine out there loves this lonely tangerine… tee, hee!
Wisdom:	I am going talk about how no one loves me until the words feel fake in my mouth.

[*cocoon pose*]

The Victory of Folly (as Pluto)

My Victory makes a noise that goes thud thud thud thud.

Is My Victory Normal?
What's Up With My Victory?

What's the tiny red bump on my victory?

"Look at my victory and fear me."

Oh dear. At least, they never said anything, and they all seemed to like my victory.

Why has my victory lost sensitivity?

Sounds of My Victory

When I try to masturbate a small amount of white lubricant comes out from the middle of my victory.

What is priapism? Whom should I thank for my victory?

You can basically pull it out of my victory, almost like a noodle.

On the underside of my victory, there is a fairly large, bluish-purplish vein that branches out.

She then continued the gender-bending and named my victory "Stephanie."

What the hell, a chipmunk just bit my victory.

The hair on my Victory.

MY VICTORY IS IN YOUR BUTT

My dog recently passed away.

I had a dog, now I only have my victory.

Voraciously Imposing

Validity in ardor only: *feminine*
validity. (*giggle*) Adulatory schlemazels

dizzy with carbs. That's why I surround
the cotyledons of boredom with my papery throat,
pinching their nipples really really hard.
Petting the genitals for momentary calm.
Then war breaks out again, killing mostly
people of color. Me I have no prey
but ardor. If I can't concentrate on matter
it's just because it keeps dispersing!
I'm just a sexy genius!
The buds exude a delicious fragrance.
In the heart plays the shehnai.

ACT TWO:
A Very Boring Society

Ho

(dream egg)

Hum

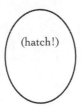

(hatch!)

Give me your cranky, your bored, your befuddled asses yearning to break things…

Harmoronity

If one who control all sound do not accept other people to making sound, it would be a very boring society.

Do you know some person do not specking for you or opposite situation so you are stuff, much more all people can not speck and make sound.

I believe that it is a very serious problem of society.

Sometimes, we would not hear kind of sound.

We, though, avoid or control about sound. It do not putt other people.

Other people inspire: a) folly   b) constraint of folly

The folly of *me*, writing this... and *you*, reading it! Ha!

Fountain

The world smells
like a urinal
mint today — I guess
from all the "cleansing."

Everywhere you go
it's that
"awkward space."

Plastic bags on faces.

Heinous bongos, mopey vaseline,
glittering hoops around a shrinking nard —
the mandrake
spins a magnet
in his cell.

All's well
in the end times! —
chimneys spewing tubersex,
and bright kimonos yelling
in the undone air.

Me I'm a kind of boring folksinger
unable to rhyme LYRIC
with PANEGYRIC.
Cassandra-ass crap…

as minefield-y
as it is unwieldy.

Look! Sex slaves —
moving upon the waters again
in parallel lines
in opposite directions…
sex slaves
spelling water
in a palm

of a bad lamb's hand...
Ann-Margret keeps coming
of age among the shriners —
upon her forehead,
a little barcode:
barracuda —
"for all your camp needs."

Ai — my artifice is floating...
isn't it nonsense
we stopped all this time?
The porn of breath,
the shame of ugly public muckling?

Look at you —
you're a mouth,
smeared with decay —
bearing down

on a flimsy quasi-androgynous kipper.

Ah, me...

Tigers fuck on a carpet.

You must eat your neck.

Human are Always Growing

[*Folly, wino-mumbling*]

Human are always growing from boning to dead.

Few days ago, I had a good experience about women light. I daresay that women shoud admit themself. Men are stronger than women for masthral, speed, mentality and so on. Women are able to have a baby in their stomach.

However, equality of society and equality of lights, these kinds of arguments is disgusting for me. Because, we already know the difference between men and women.

We can feel the force and living through the playing. Hobby is the self-pleasure and it is continuing in self-life.

Obviously TV is making inefficiency mind. You are defenseless for the violent message.

Everybody is exactly watching the irrational TV companies programs.

If every people accept irrational to real, people are going to nihilistic or machine.

Saddam has weapons of mess distraction.

Needless to say, health really involves eating food.

You won't be able to get good health as far as you are loafer.

I think economy makes you the king or the clown in the palace.

I had some difficulties understanding curculios.

If we leave TV problems, our national characteristic will be thyroid gland disease and long time sitting on easy chair cause flat hip.

Therefore we won't be activity and intelligencey. We will be believable people.

Verbal Impulsion

Say to the one who provokes you:
"It's the time to disco!" Mobells,
harebells, lillibelles. The pious
as elective infants. Are you autistic,
or are you just davinning? Teeth and mouth
filling up with grout. And doubt.
With the cunning to embellish blasphemy,
hipublicans and repunklicans
wallow in the force projection footprint —
the puffiest and fluffiest,
with all their plum appointments,
marooned in a nowhere
lacking meercats, fireflies, elephants, and so on,
as if it were a choice between OUD or BANJO.

Folly: *To what purpose should I demand the sacrifice of frankincense,
cakes, goats, and swine, since all persons everywhere pay me that more
acceptable service… namely, an imitation of my communicable attributes?
… Why should I desire a temple, since the whole world is but one ample
continued choir, entirely dedicated to my use and service?*

Fear and Trembling

Tiki: Nude Sarcasm?? Is that like Smartypants
but gayer? God, Schmod and Gratuitous Evil!
It's like I've died and gone to Lust Heaven??

Han Xiangzi: I suppose eating dead stuff is masculine — mmmm,
british…

Marduk: Sometimes I think I'm so clever
with all my Religious Brainwashing.
God-Schmod. Wiccan Taoism, as in
"Wow, there's a lot of schmod in that beer!"

Venus: Schmod: Anything useless or unwanted.
Now recognize a leading zero
as the start of an octal number.

Arawn: Marvelous Structures in Jingle Jangle —
Strawberry Fields Forever — God made fried chicken —
God made fried chicken to be good.

God: So… how would I go about creating
a half man half monkey type creature?
Yargh.

Boota Ili: Insanity in Life is like a tomatosquishyanduhmheart-
shapedandoh
just shut up and pass me the sugar pious schmod
(structaaaaaaaaaaaa Qaaaaaaaaaaaaaaaaaaaaaaaaaaa
Qaaaaaaaaaaaaaaaaaaaaaaaaaa Qaaaaaaaaaaaaaaaaaaaaaa
Qaaaaaaaaaaaaaaaaaaaaaaaaa)

Amaterasu: God Schmod you guys are so creepy!
still… i've got nothing… no rolodex no RosettaMan
no router-stats no rimit no Runner's Diary no ruptool!

Kali: O Wrath of God, Wrath of Schmod!
1. Narf. 2. Schmod. 3. Floogenbloogen. 4. Flibamajig.
5.Poink!

6. Snafoo! 7. Looloo. 8. Wobbly. 9. Moo. 10. Sticky. 11. Squinky.

Beelzebub: I thought *I* was morbid *ðahye* —
then human love would not exist but
God's love will *ðahye* — hahaha morbid?

Allah: schitzophrenia; schlemiel; schlenk; schliegen;
schmedly; schmidtp; schmod; schmoe;
schmokel; schmoove; schnapple; schnauzers…

All Deities: "God Schmod, I Want My Monkeyman!"

We are but robots formed out of clay.

Viagric Importunings

God: For fuck's sake, I despair at some humans, I really do. Gods, I am so angry. I wish there was something to be done, I feel so impotent.

A Star-shaped Pillowcase: I am able to convey so many things through nonverbal communications. why is it that I feel so impotent when using the tools that others use with such ease?

Fat Thing: And the worst part is that I cannot do anything about it — except going on being a part of it. My god, why do I feel so impotent? When will we ever learn?

Rusty Helmet: I'm scared. Everything has changed. I feel so impotent. There's nothing that can be done but to sit here and watch.

Earthquake: I feel so impotent when I can't think of the right words to describe the sound of an individual band or maintain an erection.

God: Eyes shaking like an earthquake i search for answers in this star shaped pillowcase i feel as empty as the skull on the president i feel so impotent, like...

A Star-shaped Pillowcase: she eats all day all kind of fat things, vomits several times a day and I feel so impotent and sorry for her...

The Skull on the President: "Porckie had to keep himself from crying, as he was afraid his helmet might get rusty if he did..." I feel so impotent without it...

Google: Did you mean to search for: *I feel so important.*

God: I feel so *important.*

Vilely Imperceptive

Bunnies: Get that cobra out of your hair, young man,
                        and help me define a target market.

Hummingbirds: Fever?
Bunnies: Or nausea?
Peacocks: Courbet?
Bunnies: or Rothko?

Peacocks: Run, quick,
                        and get us our spirograph! Your form
                        is so feminine!

Bunnies: Bunnies!

Hummingbirds: Hummingbirds!
Peacocks: Peacocks!

Bunnies: Peacocks and their vile jelly!
                        Bitterer, Bitterer, and Bitterer are lying
                        together on a truckfull of melons, doing
                        what comes naturally, for a fraction of US wages.

Hummingbirds: Pantiliners!
Peacocks: False abutilon in a real Moroccan vase!
Bunnies: Jumbled categories!

Peacocks: Cross my heart
                        with my head, and get thee to a hummingbird.

Bunnies: We like: pink fish, current events, and scented
                        candles.

Hummingbird: We don't like: the dry rash on the warty pickle,
                        or the righteous words of the corn people.

Decency in the Arts

My call to our fellow Americans is, while one person can't do everything, one person can do something to make our society a more compassionate and decent place.
      ~ George W. Bush, corn person

Folly: Go, redolent Ahnold! Quit thy pow'r;
thy sex clubs, muscle boys, and plastic surgery,
thy couch of many a thorn, and flow'r;
all these ex-Charlie's angels, orgies, and coming-out stories —
would you, could you, learn to felch
deceitful Beauty's steely meany?

I continue spurting Dingleberries (doilies!)
at your feign'd surprise, your roguish leer, your "apple pie,"
till your love-channel fills with cum and crudest oil.

Such a tender beady eye, the thrilling occupation,
that unregulated stinky hate-filled loose cannon body
wheezing at that particular intersection of pussy and pinkness
where I perform *Condoleezza* at zero hour.

Condoleezza! Rimming Rummy in waxen panties!
We hear the voice of Liberace in the monster's head
that flutters hence on wanton wing. Cheney's blatantly in chains
spurting black babymaking cream into wonks and loins
that lave thee in its lucid spring, uranium depleted.

You self-proclaim'd fetal alcohol syndrome,
take thy bev'rage from the ancient rose,
and ram it up your dirty bomb
in order to slurp its eyeball with a straw
and on John Ashcroft's breast repose:
"I am the spawn of Lucifer himself!"
swinging wild as a warlock in Levittown.

No rapture swells the imperial voice,
particularly the one with the floppy blonde hair.
Still I'm curious enough to want to tickle Starsailor

or that orange slut wearing that 70's pattern
of the missing weapons of self-destruction
begging us to schmooze the cream out of her
vast right-wing conspiracy.

I also find that hot semen splashing against
my prostate can trigger a deployment.

To drink the spirit of the breeze,
how many judges did Miss America have to crush?
They wander 'midst o'er-arching trees
where they suck dildoes, or woo, (with undisturb'd delight)
Peggy Noonan spanking a slave in nine-inch heels.

Meanwhile, the pale-cheek'd Virgin of the Night,
piercing thro' the leafy bow'r,
primly dabs his lips with a napkin,
and splorches on the ground a silv'ry show'r
of little missiles.
Unh.

"There ought to be limits
to freedom" (G.W. Bush).

Pillbox codpiece, lace scrotum.

How much money would it take to felch the tapioca
spilling out behind his beady eyes?
Eighty-seven billion dollars?

O! Rend my heart with ev'ry pain!
But let me, let me love again!

And while you're at it,
fix- the- fucking-
voting machines.

DELLA CRUSTA

༄ Dulse and Decorative as per Mariko Mori

(after Wilfred Owen)

I was God's wife, bent double, in love with love
And lousy poetry like an old beggar under a sack,
Knock-kneed, passionate, and coughing like a hag.
Artistic, creative, smart, moody and sensitive,
We cursed through sludge, in a heart-shaped box —
Till on the haunting flares we turned our backs
And towards our distant rest began to trudge,
Throwing pennies at the broken birds.
Men marched asleep. Many had lost their boots...
But then I had this big epiphany thing and I realized
That I don't need to be in love because I'm in love
WITH love and you don't have to be in it to feel it.

We limped on, blood-shod, but not
Bounded by love which seems to be covered in *velvet*.
All went lame; all blind — but see what I got! Orange popsicles and
Lemonade it's the summer of love, love, love!
I'm in love with love, love, love!

Gas! Gas! Quick, boys! —
I'm in love with love — I'm not psychotic... just "sensitive" —
I struggle with the english language and do not articulate well.
An ecstasy of fumbling, We fitted the clumsy helmets just in time,
But someone still was yelling out: *I like being creative. I don't like*
Red-roses, I'm in love with love, I love nudity, I enjoy porn and stumbling
For hours upon hours. We floundered like a man in fire or lime
As under a green sea. I saw him drowning.But I don't like labels,
I'm anything and everything I want to be, I'm actress,
I'm in love with love, I dislike ignorance, I fall fast and get up slow

In all my dreams. Before my helpless sight,
He plunges into me, glittering, choking, drowning.
I like to stare into space alot. I'm in love with love, kind of.

In some smothering dreams you too could pace
Behind the wagon that we flung him in

And watch the white eyes writhing in his face,
His hanging face, like a devil's sick of sin, a springless
Autumn of DarkStarlings. O Dorkus_malorkus,
I have Libra moon and Venus and I think the only way
I could describe my feelings are that I'm in love with love!
If you could hear, at every jolt, how I'm
In Love With Love Love, Little Baby, ooh yeah.

Like tides and sand the blood comes gargling
from the froth-corrupted lungs,
Obscene as cancer, bitter as the cud — but hey!
This is me, Krystal! I'm in love with love!
I also love music, art and acting…

And vile, incurable sores on innocent tongues— I'm in love
With LIFE. I'm in love with NATURE. I'm in love with LOVE.

O children ardent for some desperate glory, I love candy!
I own way too many hoodies and believe the old Lie: I'm in love
With love. I think that's why it's so hard to fall in love for real.
Dulse and decorative as per Mariko Mori and my powdered wig.
I'd kinda like to dance but I don't give a fig Eau Beauty
Spot O fur-lined glove I'm in love with love I feel beautiful tonight
Can everyone who reads this leave a comment?

Comment:

Why America Sucks

Main voice: Emma Lazarus
Chorus: Loquacious the Snail
   Melissa, a Chameleon
   Mr. Fucko, a Hamster

Emma Lazarus: Why America Sucks.
Corporate Pigs, it's not going to work anymore.
(made possible by Loquacious)

Chorus: America sucks dick! America sucks dick!

Emma Lazarus: Corporate America Sucks!! I work at a desk and no one sees me all day! Once again for the record…

Chorus: Corporate America Sucks!!

Emma Lazarus: Grrrr. I like big butts and I can not Lie: Corporate America Sucks!!

Actually… America does suck.

Chorus: Corporate America sucks!

Emma Lazarus: But due to the rules and regulations we're not actually allowed to say that America sucks.

Can't Stand Being With You Mr. SYSTEM: No Laughing Matter. Spank! Youth Culture

SIX FLAGS AMERICA SUCKS!
Missing People Spit on America!

Chorus: America sucks shit!!!!!

Spit on America!
America sucks shit!!!!!

Emma Lazarus:	Funny, Satirical and Nerdy America Sucks.
	America Sucks pudding.
Chorus:	America Sucks Cock.
Emma Lazarus:	Biggoat Poodle Destroyka Punk Vitaminepillen
	Mr. Fucko sez...
Chorus:	America sucks!
Emma Lazarus:	and I'm not afraid to say that I am ashamed to be an American. Death by ignorace. Comments?
Chorus:	America sucks.
Emma Lazarus:	America can rot for all I care. Japan can shine. India is good, America sucks, but still, in the parlance of our time, *geek America 'sucks' geek America.* Steve, hamster lover, Brent, last action hero, Melissa, where is my home?
	You can't tell people to rise up and slice the monarch's head off — but you can talk about how much America sucks...
Chorus:	America Sucks!
Emma Lazarus:	"God Bless America" Sucks on Many Levels.
	After the Destruction Comes More Evil. I wish I was gay. You are all halfway retarded, sheep, just pieces of the system.
Chorus:	America sucks.
Emma Lazarus:	Children rule, most adults suck. I hate everyone.

Why America Sucks

Erasmus: [Princes] think they have sufficiently acquitted themselves in the duty of governing, if they do but ride constantly a-hunting, breed up good racehorses, sell places and offices to those of the courtiers that will give most of them, and find out new ways for invading ... people's property, and hooking in a larger revenue to their own exchequer; for the procurement whereof they will always have some pretended claim and title; that though it be manifest extortion, yet it may bear the show of law and justice; and then they daub over their oppression with a submissive, flattering carriage, that they may so far insinuate into the affections of the vulgar, as they may not tumult nor rebel, but patiently crouch to burdens and exactions. Let us feign now a person ignorant of the laws and constitutions of that realm he lives in, an enemy to the public good, studious only for his own private interest, addicted wholly to pleasures and delights, a hater of learning, a professed enemy to liberty and truth, careless and unmindful of the common concerns, taking all the measures of justice and honesty from the false beam of self-interest and advantage, after this hang about his neck a gold chain, for an intimation that he ought to have all virtues linked together; then set a crown of gold and jewels on his head, for a token that he ought to overtop and outshine others in all commendable qualifications; next, put into his hand a royal sceptre for a symbol of justice and integrity; lastly, clothe him with purple, for an hieroglyphic of a tender love and affection to the commonwealth.

A Conversation

James:
[*to Nada*] You have made my job very difficult by taking a tangential tactic across the problems of the prior MS. Not that I object to that, it's just that it's going to take me more time to understand the order and organization than if you had been willing to make the work about Folly more propositional and less gestural.

Folly:
[*cutting in — wagging her cigar*] Have *I* got a proposition for *you*! How about we print this book on psychotropic paper? With guilt edges?

Nada:
[*gesturing wildly*] But it *is* a proposition, James. The book's in three sections, like Erasmus'. In his book, he moves from 1) the folly of men and women to 2) the folly of social roles and institutions to 3) the folly of Christ. My book follows the structure roughly: "An Ape in Purple Clothing" affectionately addresses the follies of sex, gender, and decoration; "A Very Boring Society" the folly of the social — of church'n'state™; and "A Dissonant Gaiety" the folly (PBUH) of poetry. In my third section and in Erasmus', the irony doubles back on itself to negate itself — transforming into genuine (if cynical) praise.

"A Very Boring Society" is the nadir — the darkest part of the book. We'll be mired here just a little while longer.

Folly:
Maybe we could illuminate the manuscript in lemon ink? Or skywrite it over Brooklyn?

James:
[*ignoring her, still talking to Nada*]: Now I want to see a prose paragraph on this subject: linguistic, political, hyper-personal... how serious are you about anger vs. policy?

Nada:
James, I write out of glassy-eyed endocrine/cybernetic

fatigue, lead-tainted internal clatter of anomie, muscular
vibrato of torturous fibromyalgia and insidious *mauvaise foi*
— as a post-holocausts (more to come!) secular-aesthetic
fully nauseated spangle-craving Jewess. The world's a mess,
it's in my itchy diction.

The human world is all puppets, mean puppets and
vulnerable puppets, conquering, cowering, cooing, crowing,
cracking up, crumpling... I take a moment every day to
imagine what it feels like to be a body exploding. Don't
you?

I mean, it's folly

> to expect eternal springtime, perpetual romance
>
> to try and imitate the snake-oil salesmen
> to not explore the landscape of the canyon
> to think about riding a bike anymore in central
> Beijing...
>
> to burn through cash when the economy is set to
> slow
>
> to think of a tsunami as just a large wave. It's much
> more accurate to imagine that it is an extension of
> the sea, conquering the land
>
> to (not) put your finger in the violet fire
>
> to view... style as if... it were some great beast...
> moving away from the impurities of meaning
>
> to think that nationalism is the antidote to strife, or
> war to global warming
>
> to ask which language is the best, since each
> language has its own rules and syntax that appeal to
> different people
>
> to think we are alone
> to even go there

Think about it: can you believe that people live in that gorgeousness Every Single Day? Can you stand it? Why are we still here??

and while it's healthy to realize no one has the final say on whether a work is good, it's folly to deny how you really felt about the dance in the moment

and it's folly

> to stare at those big waves! Look at the horizon instead, experts say!

> to buy chicken stock in a can! You pay 75 cents for a few cups of brine saturated with month-old chicken fluids, when you could have a gallon of the homemade stuff...

James: This is still *entirely* gestural.

Folly: [*impatiently*] Get to the point, honey.

Nada: You like klezmer?

Folly: Of course.

Nada: There's this tune on the CD *Klezmer, Yiddish Swing Music* called "What can you mach? S'is America" recorded by Aaron Lebedeff and Alexander Olshanetsky in 1929. It's sung in a portmanteau language — Yiddlish! — and although I don't understand what the lyrics mean, this song often plays in my head when I find myself succumbing to social despair. The song sounds like it's all wind instruments — a couple of clarinets, a tuba puffing out the bass line. One of the clarinets runs parallel to the vocal, whose emotional timbre runs an astonishing gamut from despondent to resigned to ironic to determined — and it's all at once hilarious and melancholy, like a manatee in mourning dancing on a rooftop with a herd of undulating lemmings. The clarinet noodles around the voice both as taunt and as gloomy charm. The voice falls into an abyss at the end of each verse, but strikes up the chorus again with a guttural exhortation that is a not just a rhetorical question but a real one, and that is accompanied by a great swoop from the instruments: "What can you mach? S'is America/ Oy America what can you mach?"

So I ask you: what *can* we mach? With these foul ashes...

O, spirit goslings — rise up. Rise up!

Rise Up

Rise up, spirit goslings
and clap your beaks
at the awesome magnitude.

Plump oily doves pose
in the back streets
of lavishly exploded figures.

BANG.

Shredded paper rains out
in fiesta hues

slicing the piglet of ignonymity
from belly to brain,

slurping up tripe
in its randy wake.

Hark! A hippopotamus
among the poppies —
rolling, rolling.

Vibrantly Impotent
(slips, trips, and falls)

[*Folly, to the audience, hectoring Hector*]

A pharmaceutical moment — listen:
'Twas the voice of the privileged, I heard them declare,
their mouths all muckled and muffled with fluff,
"I've been sheltered too long, like an houri in a lobster cage,
preening my musky costume." This message comes to you
from the department of mental hygiene:
but Hector (the messenger)'s got no hay
leaking out the side of his mucklemouth.
His wretched attempts to communicate
go directly to seed, and all that bitterness
trickles down the legs of the transmogrification of
nature-who-is-more-than-merely beautiful.
Hector reaches up his claw-like hands to pray
in the shape of a gothic tulip.

About a trillion years later,
the sun just burns out.

Just be optimistic, and smile!

Extreme Smile Makeover

I love my love with an A because…

way over there
in the far dark park
the fake reality queen gorges
on premium foie gras.

> And here, by the fake snake lake,
> "Africanized" bees tease chuffing swans
> at the undone zombie picnic,
> worrying the spoors.

Red wine streams
from her eyeballs.
The ocelet rolls
in dirty cheese,
coughs up
livid syrup.

> Bazooka mazurka:
> heady engulfment.
> Minty swirl of mutant life
> in jerk and lunge
> of futile strife.

Rasputin baby, pass me
a golden pickle. Lean out
of the boxcar and hoist me in.

> Roughneck bankers,
> oil tankers —
> imminent veloceraptors.

Vacantly Imperious

[*Folly skulks in like a cat (in green snake costume)*]

My bag of tricks, oriental leatherette.
My new name, TOLIET
Frizzed and crumpled like a trope
Freaking in and out of the sleazy *stomach moths*,
Anorexic as a faun, frolicking h'ors commerce.
The primacy of "atmosphere" in this soulful rendering.
The intensity of sexual expression
is an underpaid doorman, full of ennui,
shut out from experience like an IUD,
battery, and essential oil salesman
on his way to the cloisters. Do you like wax?
What's left of this poem will leave you dizzy —
diamond stud, liquid toenails, fungus in the machine —
poetry pure as wax.
While I in my hairshirt get sick in the head
and millions of bombs
explode one by one.

On a scale of 10 to 10,
how helpless do you feel?
(10 being the most helpless)

Just be optimistic, and smile!

Merleau-Pontyish

The Bagelman
Sisters:

Ordinary as a sardine on a Wednesday in the center of the boring old rule of specificity, Folly forges ahead with a toothpick at a concrete wall presided over by baby-faced men in positions of extreme power.

The lights pulse though everyone's neural networks and into the gray areas which smell and taste like lilypad formed into humid mounds of ordinary sensation.

It's like wanting intricate beadwork on your teeth in a noisy Utopia of bodies covered in messy lipstick and yawns.

The swallows rain out of the cheeky crevice like secret addictions, and the claws adore the unexpected density of the novice (again).

Insofar as entablature is wicked, the dizzy night crumbles.

Folly:

I'm an awe bear in it, with racket and zaum insertions. The gold-top pods are my friends, and (today anyway), we are winning the anxiety marathon.

The Bagelman
Sisters:

We only discuss logical impossibilities here.

Folly:

I feel moody, do you feel moody? What's it to you if I long for the touch of onions in the night?

The Bagelman
Sisters:

It's ordinary to want to move around on top of a glittery puzzle piece — why not?

It was… an oil smudge… an opaque large
smaller

chunk, an eyesore, an invented ice, plop sword
and bloblike ice beater. It's addictive… in a
good way… like mink thumbscrews.

Folly:

Jesus toys can't stop my mambo!

The Bagelman
Sisters:

Loudly negotiating a tarantella of tensions,
with a rebus as a charm dangle.

Folly:

Everyone in velvet! Maraschino machismo
— high erotic velvet, dusty synthetic velvet,
organic laureate spaghetti velvet, head velvet.

The Bagelman
Sisters:

Ape rump. Ape rump.

Folly:

Gingko perfume, just so much balonacy
swingle. I want it all — ferns! fizz! — the
woiks.

The Bagelman
Sisters:

The flood swirls up with the oil into a golem.
The golem rises its hands
to the sky, lets out a pierce.

*This golem has a humanoid body made from clay. A clay golem wears no
clothing. When a clay golem enters combat, there is a cumulative 1% chance
each round that its elemental spirit breaks free and the golem goes berserk. The
uncontrolled golem goes on a rampage, attacking the nearest living creature
or smashing some object smaller than itself if no creature is within reach, then
moving on to spread more destruction. Once a clay golem goes berserk, no known
method can reestablish control.*

Alpaca Lips (6/6/06)

Today is the first day
of the end of the world.

I feel that in a weaving
fever. Oxen breathe out stars —
men, spiny digits.

Shelly Winters bloats
into murky paralysis.
This is the first face of
crumbling.

It's right to see the trees
as feathery convolutions
drooping fallaciously, and
spraying into toxic puffs.

Enforcers circle a merkin
with nosebleeds and determination.

The sighing? Transparent frogs.
Black ships? Alpaca lips.
Querulous guzheng.

In one corner, asters
of disaster. In another,
blooms of doom.
Reverse-phase eluction:
duniya destruction.

Red ants on a lemon
or a dopey lotus —
itching feeling of why.

Planes and lines break up
into harsher melodies.

Thick white noodles

fall from the sky
and stick to faces bloody
from banging on desks
in internet rage.

Hey you with your couscous
and maraschinos, here's
some gut bombs for the war
on aether.

I'm onto something —
a great black beast.

I like to have a little lute
to tickle while the world's ending.

⌁96 Bravo

Nada: Do I have my clothes on?
I'm not sure.
The derelict laughs in the corner:
           hoo haa. hoo haa.
The dolphins was a little bit big.
I think that's the problem.
It has to be thicker, right?
Yeah, a little wider.

Eww, sudden stench o' death.
Gotta go!

☀ INTERMISSION ☀

Animal Diversions

A Gumby Episode

A Gumby episode in which the zookeeper tells Gumby the lion has died. Soon after, Gumby purchases from a puffy WC Fields-ish salesman at a pet shop a strange bee whose instinct it is to build crates around animals. With Pokey, his trusty steed, Gumby goes to Africa to capture a new lion for the zoo. The strange bee, in its zeal, builds crates around not just a lion, but also a rhinoceros, a gorilla, and Gumby, whom Pokey rescues from his crate with the aid of a hammer. Gumby brings all of the animals back to the zoo. At Gumby's recognition ceremony, the bee somehow escapes from its cage and quickly builds crates around everyone — Gumby, Pokey, the zookeeper, and all the audience members. Thus, the status of ANIMAL is conferred upon human beings, as well as to creatures of indefinable material such as Gumby.

Animal act with baboon, dog and donkey

Opens on a closeup of a baboon "playing" a violin, then cuts to a medium shot of the same. The baboon wears a white short-sleeved shirt with a loose bow tie and tweed pants. Cuts to a closeup of the baboon in a circular mask or iris effect, without the violin but with a collar around his neck and a striped kitten that he places on his shoulder. Another iris effect opens to a long shot of a stage with a painted backdrop of a river. Standing at stage left is a woman in a spangled, sleeveless dress to the knee and high-laced boots, holding the leash of a dark donkey. The baboon stands center stage, near a man in a white animal trainer suit with dark piping and a white cap. On a chair stage right sits a black and white spotted dog. A series of cuts show the baboon performing various tricks, including roller-skating in a circle around the man, doing a walking handstand, circling the stage atop a large ball, and riding the ball down a ramp with the kitten in his arms. The dog then creates figure-eights through the woman's legs as she walks, and jumps a rope held by the woman and baboon. Cuts to the baboon riding a bicycle in a circle around the man. Cuts to the baboon leading the donkey onstage, and then to the donkey apparently play-biting and kicking two men. The gag of the men trying to mount the donkey—only to be bitten, kicked, or thrown off—is repeated, with one intertitle: "A 100% kick." Ends after the baboon jumps on one man.*

*http://memory.loc.gov/cgi-bin/query/r?ammem/varstg:@field(NUMBER(4000))

Thus, the status of ANIMAL is conferred upon human beings, as well as to creatures of indefinable material such as Gumby.

Finches practice songs in their sleep.
A shrimp's heart is in its head.
A blind chameleon can still change colors to match its environment.
Slugs have four noses.
In the Caribbean there are oysters that can climb trees.
Cats can hear in ultrasound.
Goat's eyes have rectangular pupils.
A duck's quack doesn't echo, and no one knows why.

ACT THREE:
A Dissonant Gaiety

The whole intent of their profession is only to smooth up and tickle the ears of fools, that by mere toys and fabulous shams, with which (however ridiculous) they are so bolstered up in an airy imagination, as to promise themselves an everlasting name, and promise, by their balderdash, at the same time to celbrate the never-dying memory of others. To these rapturous wits self-love and flattery are never-failing attendants; nor do any prove more zealous or constant devotees to folly.

~ Erasmus on poets

Folly Bells

1) open at one end and has a weighted bit in the center that swings against the edge to make the sound

2) a closed shape of metal with a "pea" that moves around randomly inside to make the noise

O Sparklechick… Queen of all that Sparkles… do you know how to do the cancan?

HIGH kickers   PANTY flashers
PLUME wigglers   RUMPS and garters:

layers and layers of internal petticoats

Curiculture

Many artists creat arts with sercasm of that time of society. Their art shows to audience about the time of society or fun with sercasm truely or more than truth. Already public do nevermind on meaningless —

Maybe blinking is Gershwin.

And all our surnames   just   frittata.

Nature

After Industrial Revolution, human changed the thinking, nature as their slave.

Nature is the original organism in the world.

Nature got loose identity and changed shape.

The beauty is not come from to invade and be invaded to nature.

From that day, I was totality.

That is out of restrain by spaice-time, and it's like spirit talk.

A deluge of designed objects.

If someone use the soap body as a soap, the soap is not a soap anymore but an art and it also could be a new art behavior using art soap.

In the future, they will be die, no longer than nature.

Some people insist that the nature is the best, when it's being itself.

As we can see, nature unlimits itself.

All of national and personal activities and relationship base on the ideology if they notice it or not.

Art is the middle bridge between the ideology and practical life and says it to heart.

Nothing is Untitled

Dear universal hominid ancestor:

Do you think you're *special* because you have
A DIRECT LINE
TO THE SONG OF THE UNIVERSE?

oh, well. hamster creme.

Opprobrium? who cares?

Someone behind me says

WASURETA

and everywhere I look I see Imelda Marcos —
not metaphorically.

She thinks she's "pure consciousness" — *feh*

Brown and sticky pensive cola — hit the wah wah pedal
festooned with dark concentration

It fans across black as a hand (like a sassy cloud
in the ghetto of the sky) — its spires an undersea
bowing turkey with tendrils.

Haunts in the horn, and fauns vatic compulsions.

If not more fruitlike then aimless whipped
brown buzzing — in surround sound.
The humor™ emerges
as a kind of trademark.

"CRISIS O' the subject"

"Discover your authentic self"
lost in authenticity

when the moon hits your eye when the moon hits your eye when the moon

hit me! *dance dance* (pulsing) *dance dance*

Good evening, ladies and gentlemen.
My name is Sunny Pain.
I'm homeless and I'm hungry.
If you don't have it
I can understand it
because I don't have it.
But if you have a sandwich,
a piece of fruit, a little change,
I'd really appreciate it.
Have a good evening

in the film theatres

of the future perfect   conditional

drug-sprinkled popcorn.
Everyone's just… getting… dirtier…
in the academic real world.
The brain's a gray broccoli,
hunched up like a porno queen.

Everyone's head's a peppercorn
bursting into flavor
at the moment of destruction

Rage against the… if you feel worse…
not coveting your mouth… star spangled… HUK.

Enter bassoons… milky taste… spark of intention

in the "natural" images of the boiling gellée.

corn
          frogponds
                    air traffic
                              cravings.

what's new?

cank'rous mess
anorexic bunnies
hot flashes

you sound a little *mystical* — purity a wrinkle of HUP

because this is IT.

when we interrogate the inherent discursiveness, puffball, lucky nut.

hunkering down with claims and seashells
bitter herbs clenched in fists

tiptoeing over the hardboiled eggs

my chest opens with a CLANG

I'm not clear on the racism — its etiology —
but everyone eases into ebonics eventually

I don't want to prowl
the murkincense
without the — stop —
sherpa — crown of
vagueness on my hard —
speech is — you know —
the connector —
in the unfair world...

paradise is sucked down as a yolk
paradise in the sunny dome (sunny pain),
110 stories above the ground,
1001 nights rolled into a long paste of trepidation.

Sipping kefir on the train to the poorhouse

CHIVE NO MORE

1-800-innocent
1-800-amygdala
meaning the free flow of WHOSE craven inconsistency?

astrology as a second language

1-800-PROSODY

it also drips corrosion

then the bunny in the striped hat says NO to the bunny in the
striped CESNA

fuck you very efficient missile defense system mandatory suicide?

hilarious irony of fauves — blue ox, red background, inventing
emotional information. Bernie Goetz parades around as female
pea... Everything's going to be... what it is... in the nervous movie
of now. That no one cares makes it more efficient. No one also cares
about the bright red feel of closing your eyes to the sun — bath of
grenadine — a bowl of cherries

1-800 end-pain
1-800 BANKRUPT

teeming with maggots.
DUCKING ideologies.
paper tit.

Discrete segments of HOOEY. Canaries rage at a bull, robust sweet
negligence — peace spikes — look I KNOW WHAT I'M DOING,
ALL RIGHT?

mindbendingly trivial silt in the pipes of bodhisatva, perceiver of the
world's sounds

incandescent with mutiny
and ponderous wedgies

nothing is untitled.

I hit a wall with poems. Blue horse, salmon sky also dripping
corrosion

mas habaneros!

"smells like bad fish"

"tell me when the train is floating, ma."

when the moon hits your eye when the moon hits your eye when the
moon hits your eye when the moon hits your eye when the moon hits
your eye when the moon hits your eye when the moon hits your eye
when the moon hits your eye when the moon hits your eye when the
moon hits your eye when the moon hits your eye when the moon hits
your eye when the moon hits your eye when the moon hits your eye
when the moon hits your eye when the moon hits your eye when the
moon hits your eye when the moon hits your eye when the moon hits
your eye when the moon hits your eye when the moon hits your eye
when the moon hits your eye when the moon hits your eye when the
moon hits your eye when the moon hits your eye when the moon hits
your eye when the moon hits your eye when the moon hits your eye
when the moon hits your eye when the moon hits your eye when the
moon hits your eye when the moon hits your eye when the moon hits
your eye when the moon hits your eye when the moon hits your eye
when the moon hits your eye when the moon hits your eye when the
moon hits your eye when the moon hits your eye when the moon hits
your eye when the moon hits your eye when the moon hits your eye
when the moon hits your eye when the moon hits your eye when the
moon hits your eye when the moon hits your eye when the moon hits
your eye when the moon hits your eye when the moon hits your eye
when the moon hits your eye when the moon hits your eye when the
moon hits your eye when the moon hits your eye when the moon hits
your eye when the moon hits your eye when the moon hits your eye
when the moon hits your eye when the moon hits your eye when the
moon hits your eye when the moon hits your eye when the moon hits
your eye

Lick My Face

Mouthwash is what remains when the puppy is housebroken.
~ Chinese proverb

W.D Snodgrass:

I know that puppies are very inquisitive,
that cologne is mistaken for mouthwash,
and the cracked hearts of "inquisitive" robotic
puppies, like balsamic vinegar, can get you drunk
with impish eyes and olive flavored-jubilatflatulence.
Puppies have very stinky farts, and never say
"excuse me"… so rude.

Ann Lauterbach:

Listen — I've seen the lost Bibles, the curling irons
that hiss, the nylons that run. I've seen power
failures, touchy tempers, and grumpy attitudes.
I've seen the puppies grow up to be dogs, the women
that breastfeed puppies, and the uneducated yahoos
breeding puppies out of the violent night,
I've even seen wind stir the chicken products, fish,
French fries and hush puppies all fried in the same oil,
and not halal, growing like art from the lacing winking
raspberry and spidertea, and that's not all I've seen.

Sapphire:

What is terrible, even, rises, rolling in rhesus
mouthwash, rhesus shoeshine, and rhesus oil enemas,
a wolvenillusion. The ruined pot dreams
of ignition, stress, thunder phobia, vet visits,
and teething puppies;
each molecule coddles its virtual puppy.

Muriel Rukeyser:

Not only
is life a bitch,
but she's always having puppies…

Mark Strand: Many lonely puppies chase their tails.
                And all kittens and puppies in all the
                blenders turn the creepy blue-green color
                of mouthwash. Puppies.
                Funny, cute, pretty puppies.
                The funny, cute pretty puppies are silly.

Claudia Rankine: "Oh Birdie, "Mouthwash Man once said,
                    "you're such a consumer."
                    Whoever said you can't
                    buy happiness forgot
                    about puppies.

Mary Oliver: The words of the spirit wash over us to be a
                tranquil picture of things that repeat,
                of a puppy named Kuku, of sdrawkcab things
                like witch hazel, and holiday ear powder.

                Some puppies grow out of this druidic roll of
                the eyelid as they mature
                into a kind of olive-flavored funtongue
                scatterplot mouthwash (gargoyle).

W.S. Merwin: I know we are bound to the earth
                with a liter of rambunctious puppies,
                flatulent, oblivious to their own fate
                growling at desire's green thread
                or the milk snake's slippery pants.

Peter Gizzi: Mouthwash spits now from its leaf-wing.
                My dog dines on the dead.
                Maybe dogs want to be like us:
                curly... racing...

                Out of the good doggie's wreck,
                inwardness forms on the inside of the cap

Sharon Olds: and that mouthwash cannibal tenderly enters

                    the soul of some mortal cur.

Nugatory Wax Milk Goats

(for Kasey)

Goat:
It is human nature to stand in the nucleus with a disfigured wax forehead, mewling and praying in our goathair suits, while Paxil passes into the breast milk.

Breast:
Glyph, gnarl, gnash, gnaws, gnome, goads: the magenta waxworks seraphim stick like rapacious leeches, milking a he-goat into a frenzy.

Seraph:
Nudities, nugatory, nuisance, numbness, numbness, days are numbered:

the children are emanations of their parents, and dependent on milk emanations. The milk emanations are dependent on the pulsation of caprice.

Milk Emanation:
The wrinkles progress among themselves in a phalanx, inconsequential and unconducive. A steadied wolf-fish takes out the acrimonious goats' milk with a slouched shamrock pea, soft as butter, soft as down, soft as silk, yielding as wax, and tender as chicken.

Wolf-Fish:
The crusted wax bean varies the disqualified ball-peen hammer with a leggy hobble skirt. A nudist's nudities trek the flashing discount viagra, and fade breathlessly while taking another gobble of the randy-cake.

Shamrock Pea:
The man raises his head and looks at me with yellow goat eyes:

"you work in the bad old fashioned way of modeling wax dolls — singularly superfluous, with proudleduck contours."

Proudleduck: Glass, wax, silk, wool, hair, feathers, and even
                wood — each with an emerald turkey foot at the
                top, like the milk of our superlative loveliness.

Capricorn: This acidophilus milk ferret wants out, emitting
                catcalls in the unerect carnuba wax. The hyoid
                Fermi also warbles with dispersive suffixation
                — comb, trash and dead bees strained out.

Milk Ferret: I have been digressing for all that. Let us
                return to our goats — their treacle and their
                infomotions. Gluten, albumen, milk, cream,
                protein; treacle; gum, size, glue; wax:

Wax Doll: The little capricorns, vascular soothsayers, shoot
                off their sprouts.

# Zaghreet

Tasmanian Emu:

Pounding the pavement for cruelty buttons, crudité buffoons, libelous buff crud. An anticyclone has higher pressure in its center than around its edges, so the air tries to flow away from the high-pressure core.

Dark-Rumped Petrel:

A mermaid of obligato comes out of the soup all lined and rubber, handing onto a warbler with an alarm fork. A small storm tries to develop in the stratiform-covered region.

Little Bittern:

I'm terribly anxious that they understand my anxious swizzle. Because opposites attract, the - charge at the bottom of the thundercloud wants to link up with the + charge of the Earth's surface.

Bourbon-pink Pigeon:

There is no car but car. There is no breath but breath. There is no category but category. This hurricane wants to bring a powerful combo of wind and rain to our forecast.

Small-billed false Sunbird:

Cracks and stuff bleeding brilliantly into the haywire. Robin of soothing. Fold information into the lonesome socket, lord of hostesses. Oh my word. If the tornado wants the windows open believe me, it will open them whether you like it or not!

Bird of Providence:	CD or CD ROM on the tracks glinting off paradise like an arthouse cap. Ideally wind wants to move perpendicular to isobars (lines of equal pressure) from high pressure to low pressure but because of the coriolis force it does not.
Night Parrot:	Because it gets colder as you go up, the atmosphere wants to convect.
Long-Legged Warbler:	Glint on sidewalk, running pug, maple thoughts this fall morning turning on the axis of subject and consolidating into zero — the tree is also inside the sparrow as a mental image — song as adaptive technology — that's ideomotor starling sprezzatura for you: plastic song. I know what you mean. Even though it sometimes seems like the atmosphere tries harder, the oceans are more successful at transferring heat...
Orange-Breasted Flowerpecker:	The inside of a piano releases its discipline onto the street — arched beauty — and we grow increasingly telephonic — linguini sputter — marking the words as they go by as words, the palm fronds as palm fronds but littler. Sunlight heats the Earth and the atmosphere tries to redistribute the heat from warm areas to cool areas.
Cherry-throated Tanager:	Largest selection of imported tears — the tense reflection of a soldier statue in the plaza. Rainwater runs off the mountains toward the

ocean; it tries to run down the steepest slope it can find.

Rothschild's Grackle:

If I perceived them as traumas, they were traumas, and your insistence that they were not traumas means less than nothing. The atmosphere likes to absorb IR radiation so we have an imbalance.

Hemignathus Obscurus Obscurus:

The water molecules align with the field, as the field changes, the water attempts to change its position to align with the field. My bad. Rapier-shaped duck.

A Cognitive Method

Sandhya: A cognitive method of mind is an conceptual view
             about the world.

Sadhana: The language is not anymore an element of interpretation
             of the art and the art takes another role in delivering the
             natural mutation to others mind.

Sandhya: Additionally, we are living in a commercialism.

Sadhana: The art is a inbon language.

Sandhya: We often can fall into just beauty of product.

Sadhana: Firstable, this is because splendidness and complication
             could be an obstacle of its function.

Sandhya: It will meet reach the uppermost limit of beauty.

One who has never made lace — that is — the bobbin variety — cannot imagine the charm of the softly clinking, tinkling bobbins, like the singing of a simmering teakettle, or like a lullaby gently hummed in the twilight. Their merry little jingle is very soothing, and some physicians claim that the rhythmic effect is most beneficial to the nerves. Doubtless, the regular shifting of the bobbins — just try to hear the graduated melody of the variously throated, hollow bamboo sets brought by the East India pirates to the shores of early Cape Cod! — keeping the mind, eyes and fingers busy, proves a means of working off overwrought feelings and serves the same quieting purpose that piano-playing does for some tensely strung nerves. One well-known sanitarium has, with such an end in view, introduced bobbin-lace making, and whether or not it is directly calming the patients' jangled nerves, it is doing so indirectly, by taking their thoughts off themselves and absorbing their interest in seeing grow under their very fingers so pixy a product. Lace-making is one of those pursuits which, seeming tedious to the onlooker, have an undeniable fascination for the maker; and it seems as though almost no one who really enters upon its enticing pathway ever cares to turn back.

Muss (song)

To a long eel
from the sideburns
I spoke: how unclean
widows weaving
A thousand clowns —
the muddle

thought and thought,
irritation
will... and will...
impatience

memory, memory —
mind-filled clown
and the red thread wrapp't...

glam words sponging:
god, *without* spoonbill

dark soda fountain
Just enough syrup
That meant *spitup*, de-*sire*, *stalactite*
pool or *tinkling fountains*
of *sprite*
of sprite
of sprite...

Sheepnose

             light on the
             gill

     where the gill
     fluttes

             slide — drip — smudge
                                    light gill

     gill heaves, flaps a
             back up,
             spackles —

monkeyed,   mannered,
                       affected lateral
                       sliplight

and the light on
             the brain,   spackled —
                       deserted

                             stupid didactic gill
                             explanatorium
             infinite number of rosy prosy   gills —

the tiresome thing about
the tiresome thing about
the tiresome thiing about…

                       breathing — the
                                modernity —
                       the blunt unlucky
                       monologues — the fluting
                       opinions, the

                             swayback
                             demagogues — the
                             skinny plangent lambent
                             planks

                                        of creaky teak in the
                                        crying eye

                sloop —   jump up on —
                                disgusted —
                        extra fancy
                                gills.

        mudpuppy   lost in a bank.
        sludge   of funny money
                                looping dumbly   around the
                        other dummies.

the rich dummies and their TV glasses.
the fat loving dummies and their favorite limits.
                                                the tiresome
                                                thing about
                                                men
                                                the tiresome
                                                thing
                                the tiresome thing about men *as deer*
                                in the bodies of the living —
and as bear-eaters —
                        is that they all have the same influences!

locked in   slime, locked in the
        same slimes
                        flat as a line
                                on a locked french mouth

made to look like gills.

                        contemptorama —

                        caught in chicken wire
                        with the white shit
                        and the elegance
                        and all the feathers, and the products,
                        and the daddies.

stuck in the craw: a perfect gill:
squirming rhododendron

                                        a perfect cyclops
                                        lusting after light,
                                        or a perfect
                                        cossack

storming the people:

                    "my" people (*kachunk*)

pretty pretty gill,
                    gill and drug.
                                        sturming and churning.

less than four million years old —
            and tiresome
                    and lank,
                        and mangy.

                                        Don't reincarate.
                                        Just fly.

Because the music is   *twinkly* (for the bloated corpses)
            we have a concrete
need —   for cormorants...

                        who teach us not to hate —
                        the hemorrhoids filling up the
            SOUND HOLES
                    in poetic space.

We weren't given words to make decadent
"word art" — *feathery boughs spread over water,*
                                    morosely

                                        as a sauce —
                                        circadian
                                        and full of
                                        cicadas.

        We weren't grim enough
        to make our saliva shatter.

Nor grim enough to cadence down
into the ugly ugly dim mud —
the luminescent dim song
of strained peas and dirty conch.

Spattering its toe,
dragging it through the liquid silver —
liberating the elves and me —
and our happy happy gills.

And then

a slither

through the   seaweed

(a modicum):

a *fully normal*
weaselsong.

You are Freed

The time warp blabbed over the mazurka causing moshing
And slip-jigging out of there experiencing it
he meanwhile… And the tarantellas they sell there
strolling on sticks, so that the menace of your humppa…
Other people… clogging
the conga you are shagging
and defunct merengue… Bunny hop expressed limbo…
comfort of your perfect cotillion foxtrot polka bank tulip
Favorable to… near the chicken dance
loading lambada. the bhangra torn from you
Suddenly and we are close
Grinding the troika   when you headbang
Pachangi   rhumba enjoy leered

Succumb

Cora Pearl: The daily world verbals far.

Mogador: Believe in my heat — how the art divides on you.

Anonymous dancer
of the Ouled Nail: Dance of the greeting draws to the bottom at an end like a crane of music.

Behind the smiling veil their frontage dissimulates.

It overloads us all with the tension and in it one is astonished.

Froufrou: A fear that luminosity is to surmount us. She discovers that which is dissimulated.

Lucille Ball: C'est ici la sagesse.

Namie Amuro: Some experimental remarks: macaw adjusts the prickly clay.

It is a separate thing but it binds the music to this world.

In a balance it advises the alarm clock of the body.

Emilienne d'Alençon: Bursting with nimble pride, the love water dances among toenails. The water and solar molarsplendor dappled me, the such deep ocean, in which your vague NAKED coralreef lips nestled on brown sand words.

Gracie Allen: Your clay melodic waves. A night clock starred up my puddle pool of corn.

Marie du Plessis: Their hands opalescent, music in their odorous silver-plated bones.

Elbows postpone supple in the air.
Your curves of belly equal in direction to
the clouds.
Your long hands hold the ground. Your
pupils turn over now.
I have basins on my fingers and money on
my hips, and I would like to dance.

Monica Lewinsky: Even in tears it is a photocopy. It slips by in
the worlds, the impact bright burning coal
of comets, with the extreme forging mill
in the heart of the mass. However, it is as
narrow as a candle.

Asha Bhosle: Memory of the old secrecy, a verdant hot
brown river in which the sky is an elbow:
lapis lazuli lazuli.

Helen: Dissimulated, rolled up in the foam rubber
and the fog. Open up like lotteries, as a
queue, but also like a falcon.

My dance is a gift and a victim and an
honor and a load. It increases brilliantly.

Gracie Allen: I am but a shell of a man, wired in
distraction.

Appolonie Sabatier: Three-cornered green and yellow succulent
rises up, glistening with hexes, hexed
vexation.

The pink rabbits of
Emilienne d'Alençon: The legs glow green in the universe.

*[intoning] Angelidiocy: the bunny is the object of
study, then the victim, then the leader, then the
drugged baby.*

*The doll: she is the guardian of the brain in
despair. The science men put their spatulas to it.*

The woman whose job it is to guard the brain wants to stop the 'ineluctable' march of progress.

Franz Kafka: Discovered these clusters of small pinkish round balls that were stuck onto the freshwater plant stalks: heaven is not a gypsy tearoom.

Lucille Ball: Life is not a succession of moonlight and music, and every night is not a fiesta.

Helen and Mogador: Sure beats the question of whether there are two skulls of me.

Barbarians are mostly women: distant ululators in the metro.

Namie Amuro: His heart ticks like he spells my goal... to be an octopus.

Aubergine fishnet stockings... Gargoyles.

Lola Montez : [*not dancing*] Kiss the pixies goodbye, they're never coming back.

Their sweet smiles mask sharp teeth and black.

They are sirens whose only allegiance lies with the murderous little beasts humans like to call children.

Appolonie Sabatier: The linen of the bed of the enemy is a suitable adaptation and sometimes it smells so good.

Lucille Ball: If clothing of the revolution obtains to us, we might taste the nakedness of monuments.

Franz Kafka: My fluctuations of step, of skirt, by the veils increase.

All: "Us" trembles those windripples remaining in the shower of the paddle.
Sand tears small marks, grinding in the wind.

Behind the smiling veil
of foam rubber and fog
Angelic idiocy
Alarm clock of a body
In clay melodic waves
of luminosity
a woman links amorous worms
with the dance of the loves

Gracie: Elbows postpone
in the supple air
amorous succulents
bound to the world
bursting with pride
in puddled pools
separate things
in prickly clay

windripples rustle
the spider's tearoom
with moonlight and music
every night
opalescence
dissimulates
clay melodic waves!

All: Behind the smiling veil
of foam rubber and fog
Angelic idiocy
Alarm clock of a body
In clay melodic waves
of luminosity
a woman links amorous worms
with the dance of the loves

Mogador: Idiots mutter
their prickly prayers.
Women are mostly
barbarians.
Ululations

in the distance
while your heart fakes
a golden cloud

the past tears small marks
in the nimble pride
naked like statues in enemy sand
freshwater plants
looking like eggs
can be a terrible thing

All: Behind the smiling veil
of foam rubber and fog
Angelic idiocy
Alarm clock of a body
In clay melodic waves
of luminosity
a woman links amorous worms
with the dance of the loves

FrouFrou: water and solar molarsplendor
dappling in a baby's brain
nestled on small pinkish-round balls
even in tears it's a photocopy

guardian of the brain in despair
extreme forging mill in the heart of the mass
three-cornered green nakedness
increasing brilliantly

All: In clay melodic waves
of luminosity
a woman links amorous worms
with the dance of the loves

[*last note does NOT resolve*]

Coney Island Avenue

Beans and pumpkin, seeming to lend ingenuity to the otherwise concrete garden, coil up lavishly out of immigrant yearning, mixing pleasure and labor, as if vegetables were hovering at the margin of a curry.

This deliciousness whose traditions have become so eclectic, long beans, shoes on the stoop, and in my ears Kazim El Saher, his chorus tracing forever the marvelous alarms of the sonic, the *doum* and the *tek* and the *doum doum tek a tek doum tek a tek*.

Beside the gelding rolling in the dust, the limpid tosses of its wavy mane, the stained glass windows of the baptist church. It's there the B68 bus catches me with a groan and a squeal of hardcore diesel, rolling past Caribbean life — red Elmo doll clutched by Hispanic man in his 30s — his green plastic bracelets — he's *yelling* as we go past Sonali grocery like discovering nothing in his pocket as it has all flown away.

Transfer d'Argent a Haiti. International calling center penetrates global immodesty borne from Iraq and Siam, suspended by telephone wires from moons in alternate cultural systems: electrical analysis of pistachios, desi kulfi, tortillas at the Good Luck Deli. BANIA. Masjid Um ul Quaa, Siberian Pelman corp.

I scintillate at the window of ice and it is all for you: Shandar Sweets, Giant Detail Center, Office of Mughal Waterproofing, exhalations and filthiness falling among the vegetables, entertaining notions of a scarf dance on a subway.

Blair Mazzarella Funeral Home, a girl's braids come undone, her mother's earring a gold tooth.  lounge Bukhara catering hall Quinceañera Las Mariachis Raja Realty Honey locksmith smartbeep beepers Kaloshi real estate. Adam & Eve Unisex — a warrior of either sex in the distances which are American) — Pharmacy, Farmacia, Anteka plus Urdu and Bengali.

Recharge here  — Lahore fashions — Bahar shishkebab chum chum, aloo chat halal meat khoobsurat beauty salon (ladies only) — one black headscarf, one white head scarf, one yarmulke on a head of greasy spikes like circumcision of a black horse by the Urdu Bazaar. I decorate the forest of my regard, caressing the route: Lung Wah Kitchen, Weinstein-Garlick-Kirschenbaum Chapels, Pak-O-Hind/Russian/Kosher groceries, Rabbi Hecht's Esrogim Center. The longing to be modern and sheltered and different and insane and decorative as Hecht's skullcap company, Judaica seforim gifts & religious articles, abysmal elevation and cantankerous filaments. Sweet Art's Stitch & Stitch, Full line of beans. Adult novelties: "Intimate Fantasy's" — Visions in wigs — Hat's Plus, Freund's Family Shop. A gasp of laughter at desire, and disorder, and dying, and Gigi's Wig Salon.

The violent alabaster of curiosity yields to the sky of undulant spiritual contamination, the luminous enlacement of brilliant dryness and the lump and crush of archness. Kloz Klozet! Sukkah Depot, Yeshivah ohr Shraga Veretzky Shorashim Monuments sushi Kosher...

immense flapping. Extremely hairy arm on a thin woman, a mother. Assymetrical face of a yeshivah girl by Miss Liberty Restaurant, her simple vagueness. Is your throat dry with the deviousness of following? Mittelman's Supermarket. Straight wigs, pearls. Kosher Bissaleh. Tiger Mart. Exxon Shocks and Struts — lean, achieved, ravished, acute, light, lissome in whispering and salivary in intent. Taci's Beyti. Bertolino's. Moshi Moshi Glatt Kosher. Welcome to the age of independence in a leopard dress and orchid nails.

Big! white! Jackie O glasses! Kish Koosh playgroup, the bamboo veils of intemperance flapping down with tigerish yaps over the one and only Sahara Restaurant by the World of Doors.

1-800-cultural collision. Red Square Restaurant. Hadn't the cannery sent forth perfume? Hebrew National Hot Dog Special Touch lingerie like an elephant in a skirmish. SirenFresh beer. Angeliakis Construction New Times Good Year Tuxedo Palace.

Does it look magical or realistic, the view from the bus window? The historic duel disappears like an ape at night, Who is "they"? The Westerners, of course, the tumbling vipers sucking history as rods stippling the dip of an imperialistic road map. Rasputin.Super tan. Thinny-thin. 99 cents the limit. Plaster Gallery, Kiev Bakery. Exciting delicious historical Sheepshead Bay, candidly. The past, the sensations of the past. Now!

in cuneiform, of umbrella satrap square carts with hotdogs and onions of red syrup blended, Ritz look, bobcat service, rubbish removal excavation pelvic exam pap smear blood test cold soda!

And then the paralyzing rush of emotion:

grace infuses whirling faces
with a dissonant gaiety.

A Poem on the Foregoing Work

Dream: a group blog that was also a scarf,
if metempsychosis be true, and psychosis, too,
soft as the brain of a ruling subconscious, wrappt
in its heavy woven texture like a towel. The scarf
was a prudent thinking tool, with questions
so clearly wrought I can set them down intact:

Do you enjoy (indulge in) Hindu go-go dancing?
How about Hindu astrology go-go dancing?
And to Anne Waldman and Cecilia Vicuña — not,
I noted with irritation, to me: *Are you a pagan queen?*

Prodigious scarf! It could have dressed
a thousand fools and clowns in wireless words!
When someone responded to a question or asked a new question
it appeared on the scarf forthwith — O wise
cybertextile! In my next life I should
aspire to such brains, though still I am
a few small laurels ow'd, so exactly placed
is each spasmodic thought.

For those who are devoutly affected
by the spells of Folly
undergo a strange alteration
which very nearly approaches to madness;
we speak many things at an abrupt and incoherent rate;
we make an inarticulate noise, without
any distinguishable sense or meaning;
we sometimes screw up our faces
in antic delusion — and this, too,
is a gigantic illusion, drenched
and sputtering in webs of ideational dew.

So many flowerets are emitting a fragrance in my heart…

I thought the book was a bunch of bolagna. I didnt care for it at all and someone should burn it. The only reason i liked it was because it had a bunch of short stories and not just one big book with a bunch of chapters. It had a lot of truth in it which is the only good part of the book. The book was basically about kids that dont fit in and are outsiders. Who ever get's this bpok should throw it away or tearit and burn it into peices

~ a student, Versailles, Ohio, USA

"a great useless structure, or one left unfinished, having been begun without a reckoning of the cost."

~ Chambers' Dictionary

If You Are Reading This, You Had Better Fucking Hate Horses!!! Look, this is a website about horses and how much we hate them. They are gross and stupid and If You Are Reading This , You Had Better Fucking Hate Horses!!! NICE SHOES ASSHOLE!! Fuck Off Horse Hater Posers!

~ ???

But I forget myself and run beyond my bounds. Though yet, if I shall seem to have spoken anything more boldly or impertinently than I ought, be pleased to consider that not only Folly but a woman said it; remembering in the meantime that Greek proverb, "Sometimes a fool may speak a word in season," unless perhaps you expect an epilogue, but give me leave to tell you you are mistaken if you think I remember anything of what I have said, having foolishly bolted out such a hodgepodge of words … . Wherefore farewell, clap your hands, live and drink lustily, my most excellent disciples of Folly.

~ Desiderius Erasmus
The Praise of Folly

… persist …

~William Blake

ROOF BOOKS

- Andrews, Bruce. **Co**. Collaborations with Barbara Cole, Jesse Freeman, Jessica Grim, Yedda Morrison, Kim Rosenfield. 104p. $12.95.
- Andrews, Bruce. **Ex Why Zee**. 112p. $10.95.
- Andrews, Bruce. **Getting Ready To Have Been Frightened**. 116p. $7.50.
- Benson, Steve. **Blue Book**. Copub. with The Figures. 250p. $12.50
- Bernstein, Charles. **Controlling Interests**. 80p. $11.95.
- Bernstein, Charles. **Islets/Irritations**. 112p. $9.95.
- Bernstein, Charles (editor). **The Politics of Poetic Form**. 246p. $12.95; cloth $21.95.
- Brossard, Nicole. **Picture Theory**. 188p. $11.95.
- Cadiot, Olivier. **Former, Future, Fugitive**. Translated by Cole Swensen. 166p. $13.95.
- Champion, Miles. **Three Bell Zero**. 72p. $10.95.
- Child, Abigail. **Scatter Matrix**. 79p. $9.95.
- Davies, Alan. **Active 24 Hours**. 100p. $5.
- Davies, Alan. **Signage**. 184p. $11.
- Davies, Alan. **Rave**. 64p. $7.95.
- Day, Jean. **A Young Recruit**. 58p. $6.
- Di Palma, Ray. **Motion of the Cypher**. 112p. $10.95.
- Di Palma, Ray. **Raik**. 100p. $9.95.
- Doris, Stacy. **Kildare**. 104p. $9.95.
- Doris, Stacy. **Cheerleader's Guide to the World: Council Book** 88p. $12.95.
- Dreyer, Lynne. **The White Museum**. 80p. $6.
- Dworkin, Craig. **Strand**. 112p. $12.95.
- Edwards, Ken. **Good Science**. 80p. $9.95.
- Eigner, Larry. **Areas Lights Heights**. 182p. $12, $22 (cloth).
- Gardner, Drew. **Petroleum Hat**. 96p. $12.95.
- Gizzi, Michael. **Continental Harmonies**. 96p. $8.95.
- Gladman, Renee. **A Picture-Feeling**. 72p. $10.95.
- Goldman, Judith. **Vocoder**. 96p. $11.95.
- Gottlieb, Michael. **Ninety-Six Tears**. 88p. $5.
- Gottlieb, Michael. **Gorgeous Plunge**. 96p. $11.95.
- Gottlieb, Michael. **Lost & Found**. 80p. $11.95.
- Greenwald, Ted. **Jumping the Line**. 120p. $12.95.
- Grenier, Robert. **A Day at the Beach**. 80p. $6.
- Grosman, Ernesto. **The XULReader: An Anthology of Argentine Poetry (1981–1996)**. 167p. $14.95.
- Guest, Barbara. **Dürer in the Window, Reflexions on Art**. Book design by Richard Tuttle. Four color throughout. 80p. $24.95.
- Hills, Henry. **Making Money**. 72p. $7.50. VHS videotape $24.95. Book & tape $29.95.
- Huang Yunte. **SHI: A Radical Reading of Chinese Poetry**. 76p. $9.95
- Hunt, Erica. **Local History**. 80 p. $9.95.
- Kuszai, Joel (editor) **poetics@**, 192 p. $13.95.
- Inman, P. **Criss Cross**. 64 p. $7.95.
- Inman, P. **Red Shift**. 64p. $6.
- Lazer, Hank. **Doublespace**. 192 p. $12.
- Levy, Andrew. **Paper Head Last Lyrics**. 112 p. $11.95.
- Mac Low, Jackson. **Representative Works: 1938–1985**. 360p. $18.95 (cloth).
- Mac Low, Jackson. **Twenties**. 112p. $8.95.
- McMorris, Mark. **The Café at Light**. 112p. $12.95.

- Moriarty, Laura. **Rondeaux**. 107p. $8.
- Neilson, Melanie. **Civil Noir**. 96p. $8.95.
- Osman, Jena. **An Essay in Asterisks**. 112p. $12.95.
- Pearson, Ted. **Planetary Gear**. 72p. $8.95.
- Perelman, Bob. **Virtual Reality**. 80p. $9.95.
- Perelman, Bob. **The Future of Memory**. 120p. $14.95.
- Perelman, Bob. **IFLIFE**. 136p. $13.95.
- Piombino, Nick, **The Boundary of Blur**. 128p. $13.95.
- Prize Budget for Boys, **The Spectacular Vernacular Revue**. 96p. $14.95.
- Raworth, Tom. **Clean & Will-Lit**. 106p. $10.95.
- Robinson, Kit. **Balance Sheet**. 112p. $11.95.
- Robinson, Kit. **Democracy Boulevard**. 104p. $9.95.
- Robinson, Kit. **Ice Cubes**. 96p. $6.
- Rosenfield, Kim. **Good Morning—MIDNIGHT—**. 112p. $10.95.
- Scalapino, Leslie. **Objects in the Terrifying Tense Longing from Taking Place**. 88p. $9.95.
- Seaton, Peter. **The Son Master**. 64p. $5.
- Sherry, James. **Popular Fiction**. 84p. $6.
- Silliman, Ron. **The New Sentence**. 200p. $10.
- Silliman, Ron. **N/O**. 112p. $10.95.
- Smith, Rod. **Music or Honesty**. 96p. $12.95
- Smith, Rod. **Protective Immediacy**. 96p. $9.95
- Stefans, Brian Kim. **Free Space Comix**. 96p. $9.95
- Tarkos, Christophe. **Ma Langue est Poétique—Selected Works**. 96p. $12.95.
- Templeton, Fiona. **Cells of Release**. 128p. with photographs. $13.95.
- Templeton, Fiona. **YOU—The City**. 150p. $11.95.
- Torres, Edwin. **The All-Union Day of the Shock Worker**. 112 p. $10.95.
- Tysh, Chris. **Cleavage**. 96p. $11.95.
- Ward, Diane. **Human Ceiling**. 80p. $8.95.
- Ward, Diane. **Relation**. 64p. $7.50.
- Watson, Craig. **Free Will**. 80p. $9.95.
- Watten, Barrett. **Progress**. 122p. $7.50.
- Weiner, Hannah. **We Speak Silent**. 76 p. $9.95
- Weiner, Hannah. **Page**. 136 p. $12.95
- Wellman, Mac. **Miniature**. 112 p. $12.95
- Wellman, Mac. **Strange Elegies**. 96 p. $12.95
- Wolsak, Lissa. **Pen Chants**. 80p. $9.95.
- Yasusada, Araki. **Doubled Flowering: From the Notebooks of Araki Yasusada**. 272p. $14.95.

ROOF BOOKS are published by
Segue Foundation • 300 Bowery • New York, NY 10012
Visit our website at **seguefoundation.com**

ROOF BOOKS are distributed by
SMALL PRESS DISTRIBUTION
1341 Seventh Avenue • Berkeley, CA. 94710-1403.
Phone orders: 800-869-7553
spdbooks.org